Women and Early Christianity

Women and Early Christianity

Are the feminist scholars right?

Susanne Heine

SCM PRESS LTD

Translated by John Bowden from the German
Frauen der frühen Christenheit,
published 1986 by Vandenhoek and Ruprecht, Göttingen.

© Vandenhoeck and Ruprecht 1986

Translation © John Bowden 1987

British Library Cataloguing in Publication Data

Heine, Susanne
Women and early Christianity: are the feminist
scholars right?
1. Bible. N.T. — Criticism — interpretation etc.
2. Women in Christianity   3. Bible and feminism
I. Title   II. Frauen der frühen Christenheit
English

225'.01   BS2370

ISBN 0-334-02423-4

First published in English 1987
by SCM Press Ltd
26-30 Tottenham Road, London N1

Phototypeset by Input Typesetting Ltd
and printed in Great Britain by
Richard Clay Ltd
Bungay, Suffolk

Contents

After the Outcry

1. In 1971 Elizabeth Gould Davis's book *The First Sex* appeared. To begin with, it did not attract much attention, but two years later it had become a classic of the feminist movement since, as the publishers claimed, 'it is inspiring, illuminating and true in the authentic sense of truth'.[1]

'The first males were mutants,' Davis wrote.[2] 'Freaks produced by some damage to the genes, caused perhaps by disease or a radiation bombardment from the sun... The suspicion that maleness is abnormal and that the Y chromosome is an accidental mutation boding no good for the race is strongly supported by the recent discovery by geneticists that congenital killers and criminals are possessed of not one but two Y chromosomes, bearing a double dose, as it were, of genetically undesirable maleness. If the Y chromosome is a degeneration and a deformity of the female X chromosome, then the male sex represents a degeneration and deformity of the female.'[3]

In 1983, just over ten years later, a dissertation appeared from the Catholic theologian Manfred Hauke entitled *The Problems of the Priesthood of Women against the Background of Creation and Redemption.*[4] Hauke, too, used chromosomes to prove his thesis: '...in the sex chromosomes the female is to some degree contained in the male (X in XY). Thus in theory it would be possible to produce a female chromosome from the male by duplication of the X chromosome but not vice versa. To some degree the woman has come "out of" the man. The Y chromosome seems almost to be the symbol of transcendence.'[5] Therefore by nature women are not fitted for the priesthood.

This is a controversy which at least makes one chuckle, but such a reaction ignores too easily what largely determines the 'war of the sexes'. Both authors lay claim to a biological argument to substantiate, if not to 'prove', their dominant interest. The woman stamps all men as criminal, at least potentially, while the man declares all women to be weak-minded creatures who are lost to transcendence.

Does not Davis know that the duplication of the X chromosome leads to weak-mindedness? Do not both of them know that chromosome chains are hardly equipped to be a basis for theological statements?

Grotesque as all this may seem, in many ways it is symptomatic of what is taking place in the debate over feminist theology: the working out of terrifyingly simple prejudices. 'All men are...', 'all women are...' keeps being said, and not just in the two publications which I have cited. The series of books in which prejudices are almost shamelessly 'substantiated' in a pseudo-scientific way could be continued on both sides.

If we apply the criterion of what characterizes those who are governed by, indeed steeped in, prejudice, a good deal of feminist literature is no different from the 'masculine' literature against which it fights. Stereotypes, the formation of intellectual and social cliques, distorted perception as a result of excessive emotional involvement, boosting personal prestige – criticism is always made only of the other side – , an inability to differentiate and to see that the light and dark sides cannot be distinguished so clearly, a complete lack of self-criticism, in short a concentrated defence of anything that is different, especially if this is felt to be alien.[6] Behind all this one can trace anxiety, feelings of impotence and weakness, which become even more striking when women and men enter into the 'noble' contest to see which of the two is the more persecuted, the poorer, the more deceived.

2. Now we should certainly not overlook the fact here that there are victims among women and men, increasingly more among women. For centuries there have been prejudices against women, and mental and physical violence has been done to them. It is possible for them to state this, to make it public, to seek support for themselves in the way that ethnic and religious minorities do when they are denied humane treatment, and that has proved an effective political course. But where this is again combined with prejudices which are now against the other side,

the humanizing that they expect and call for cannot take place, and the battle becomes all the more fatal. The battle must be against all prejudices, and not for the imposition of a different, new prejudice.

Tilmann Moser's book *The Poisoning of God*[7] caused quite a stir when it appeared. Here was an expression of his suffering by someone who had been psychologically damaged by Christian education and the social life of the church. But without rejecting the gravity of such suffering we might nevertheless ask whether we are to conclude from this that Christian faith and the church must necessarily damage people. Empirically, what Tilmann Moser says will apply not only to him, but also to many others who grew up in such an environment. But what does this prove? It is also empirically possible to demonstrate a healthy influence of Christianity and a great deal that is unhealthy in the secular sphere. Empiricism always 'proves' everything; it is never clear and either 'positive' or 'negative' in itself. To close one's eyes to negative experience does not make things different any more than does putting stress on this experience, fixing one's attention on it. Only if we leave the empirical level and consider the Christian claim, only where there is a concern for love, trust and forgiveness, is there also associated with it the task of proving this claim in practice and thus shaping and altering reality.

By way of comparison that also goes for the fraught relationship between women and men. No one can want to talk someone out of disastrous experiences, to make these a matter of moral reproach or attribute them to a lack of vitality. All that would be cynical. Support is needed towards those who have been hurt. But even that cannot be justified in empirical terms or be 'proved' necessary; it remains a humanitarian claim and belongs in the sphere of ethics, including Christian ethics.

3. One of the greatest problems of feminism and feminist theology seems to me to lie in the fact that women form a negative theory out of their hurt and their negative experience and claim universal validity for it. It is then the 'nature' of the male to be destructive, the 'nature' of the Christian tradition to damage people, to eliminate women from history, to demonize the feminine. This absolutizing of negative experience, even though – it must be acknowledged – it is largely dominant, creates prejudice

and weakens ethical claims. Such a 'frenzy of the negative' (Hegel) leads to a paralysis of all ideas and thus too of any attempts at change. Anyone who studies the history of women in the Christian tradition will come upon a great deal which goes against the claim of Christian faith. And yet, anyone who therefore gives up the baptismal formula in Gal.3.28, that in Christ there is neither man nor woman, confirms the history of contradiction, rather than offering a critical challenge to it. Those prejudiced theories are particular dangerous which garb themselves in scientific methods and in so doing confirm the necessity of negative experience and destruction. If the Y chromosome is 'guilty' of the criminal tendencies of the male, what else can be expected of males than that they should do violence to females? So women fight against traditional prejudices and in so doing often replace a negative prejudice with a positive one or produce new negative prejudices among their opponents – thereby damaging themselves.

4. Any kind of prejudice needs to be contradicted. Only when this happens does a constructive development in the difficult 'man-woman problem' seem to be possible. I am not saying that this would be easy. How do you deal with prejudices? Enlightment as to their bad effects? Moral appeals? Canvassing for emotional understanding for the other side? Psychotherapy for those with weak egos? Education aimed at eliminating prejudices? Whatever the suggestion, Theodor Adorno has kept pointing out that 'we have to deal not only with people whom we can shape and change but also with those in whom the die is already cast, often those whose particular personality structure is characterized by being in some way hardened, who are not really open to experience, not really flexible: in short, people you cannot talk to.'[8] And Adorno does not rule out the possibility that one has to be 'militant' against such people, militant being understood not as a desire to punish, but as 'moral power'.[9]

However we are to estimate the various courses and their possible success, I see no other alternative than to attack prejudices, no matter on which side they appear and are brought into play; this is the only possible way of getting out of the vicious circle of each side blaming the other, and also of being able to live with those aspects of reality which seem strange and threatening, so that they can lose their threatening character and be felt as an enrichment.

5. I want to attempt that from my own context, that of the academic world, whose disciplines can play a disastrous role as a 'proof' for prejudices. The so-called results of scholarship, the historicity of which can easily be overlooked, are readily claimed as authoritative support for one's own wishes, which then form the principle of selection. Over against this I would set an understanding of scholarship which begins from an awareness of its limitations: there is a particular method for every object which produces a corresponding result. Every method begins from a heuristic interest which determines the results and which must also be taken into account for the sake of exactness. Exactness is always the specific feature of science and scholarship. But that all remains embedded in prior interests, and the relevance of the results for the world in which people live. The objectification of interests, the abandoning of what is empirically to hand, the questioning or reasons, the question of the 'truth' as something that is universally valid, in other words scientific reflection on various levels, may well include the provision of answers which are unacceptable, which people do not want to be given. That too can be a decisive contribution against the bonds of prejudice.

6. A survey of feminist theological literature shows a striking contrast in its assessment of the Christian tradition. Here Christianity, especially beginning with Paul, is made responsible for any hostility to women. A corresponding selection of texts provides evocative evidence of this. There Christianity has its roots in Jesus of Nazareth, the 'feminine' man, who through his erotic relationship with Mary Magdalene did away with all discrimination against femininity. What is left of Paul, who fought alongside women for the gospel? What is left of Jesus, who does not speak specifically of women and who went around with his followers, men and women, without having a fixed abode and without possessions, and who spoke harsh words against family ties?

There is no doubt that a history of Christian hostility to women can be written, but so too can a history of Christian friendliness towards women. From where are we to derive the criterion for judging which side is genuinely Christian? And even if it could be shown that the tradition hostile to women was the more developed one, that is far from saying that this must be, should be, the characteristic of Christianity.

So I am concerned with exactness, and in it I see the contribution of scholarship to this theme: exactness in the historical and systematic-theological sense; exactness in discerning methods and making a critical estimation of what they can and what they cannot do in any particular situation.

7. Here I come to a second decisive problem which I perceive from feminist literature: the acknowledgment of 'Methodicide'.[10]

This slogan is used to interpret scientific methodology as the virile compulsion of a system. Feminine emotion is contrasted with 'male theology of the head' and said to contradict it. The immediate experiences of women give the answer to the 'male business' of abstract thought. Theory and practice are assigned to men: the one here, the other there. It is not just that this fuels a further prejudice, that women are not sufficiently endowed with intellect; this kind of polarization is endorsed by the dominance of the empirical, natural-scientific method in science which cannot be overcome with emotions.

Today the thought-models of the natural sciences have also largely become established in the humane sciences and are regarded as decisive, though critical voices have gained an increasing hearing. Instead of challenging science, theory-forming and method in principle, which would amount to refusing to think at all, it is really necessary to reflect even more exactly, to distinguish methods, to ask which methods are appropriate for which subjects, and which results are to be expected. The lack of clarity in distinctions leads to false judgments and circular arguments, and in this way again favours prejudices and dogmatisms.

I have already shown that while experience is to be taken seriously in personal terms, no principles of general validity can be derived from it, not even where the frequency of an experience seems to suggest this. In principle things can always be different. Thus for example many women complain that the Christian confession of God as Father has led them to turn away from faith and the church because of their destructive experience of their own father. So they propose 'doing away with' the Father God in favour of the 'Mother God'. However, the same argument can be applied again in the new circumstances. Personal, possibly destructive experiences of one's mother can now in turn hinder approach to a feminine deity and again be made responsible for people 'having to' turn away from faith and the church. So experience can never be proof of the binding character of a statement of faith. So we need to think more clearly, in exact methodological reflection, about the relationship between experience and confession or how the statement 'God is Father' is valid.

8. A further problem of method is posed by historical research, which has an established place in theology, especially in exegetical disciplines. As a rule historical criticism is practised according to the principle of Leopold von Ranke, 'as it really happened'. Underlying this is the claim to be making generally valid statements about what 'in fact' happened. However, as theological texts are above all concerned with the motivations behind human faith, the historical-critical method can only be applied to such texts to a limited degree, since the questioning specifically leaves aside such motivation.[11] Thus the New Testament texts show, for example, that there were women around Jesus (Luke 8.1-3). However, at the least there can be a dispute as to what this means, and that can also be demonstrated from the literature. Were these women followers of Jesus in the comprehensive way that the disciples were, or did they provide financial support and a limited degree of *diakonia* for Jesus and his followers?[12] The text, at least, gives no clear answer, and that means that it escapes the intended exactness of the historical method, where that is understood as being an individual discipline.

If we assume – and that in turn is already a hypothesis and not an exact result – that women and men were followers of Jesus to an equal degree, what does that mean for the present position and function of women in the Christian churches? Jesus and the traditions which tell of him were regarded within the churches, particularly the Reformation churches with their scripture principle, as the authority and criterion for judging what is 'right' in a Christian sense. Without such authority, i.e. in a secular context, this cannot be established, which means that the present and not the past praxis of the churches attests what is decisive for them. But that means in turn that historical research can produce something relevant to practice only on the presupposition that Jesus is confessed as the criterion of Christian self-understanding. Historical criticism in itself cannot recover from an analysis of the Jesus tradition any generally binding and valid statement for an assessment of the role of women.

9. Where the biblical texts are taken as canonically valid, however, Jesus and his praxis are the criterion for the praxis of Christians. No historical research is needed for such a statement. If this is taken into account, the question again arises as to 'how things really were'. If women and men were in fact equally disciples, we would have to investigate the conditions in which this was the case: detached from the traditional forms of society, without a fixed abode, without possessions, dependent on alms and provisions from those who were 'sedentary', these people travelled from place to place. There is no mention of family, children, household. Whether they also practised sexual asceticism is at least an open question which is very difficult to answer. What does this say nowadays for women today in church and community? Does not the world around Jesus of Nazareth remain an utterly strange one? What if it emerges from this that women disciples, in so far as the historical form of this discipleship is taken quite seriously, are conceivable only in unusual social circumstances? We are again up against questions which historical research cannot answer.

Mutatis mutandis the same considerations also apply to the discussion of the significance of women in Gnostic communities. In so far as we can obtain any historical information, women seem to have had much more preferential positions in the Gnostic communities and were much less limited in their functions than in the so-called orthodox communities. Anyone who detaches such an individual motive from the overall context of a Gnostic thought system may regret the success of the battle of the early church against Gnosticism.[13] Anyone who takes the overall context into account will also come up against the suspicious result of the rigidly ascetic practice of the Gnostics, which also raises questions for their estimation of women.

10. Feminist interest outside theology and within has set to work on re-examining and continuing the research into matriarchy carried on in the nineteenth century. Given the scarceness

of sources from the time before about 1000 BC, it is difficult to gain an authentic picture of the period. The difference between the exactness of the method and the vagueness of the sources can be seen even more clearly here than in the analysis of the beginnings of Christianity. But even supposing that we assume that there were matriarchies and a subsequent patriarchal revolution, what does that say for assessing the historical evidence, especially as the historical evidence cannot *a priori* escape the making of a value judgment? Bachofen speaks of progress in history, feminists speak of a regress. If emotional and therefore arbitrary interests do not lie behind this difference, if any universally valid statement can be made about it, it is necessary to resort to another 'object' and apply a method other than the historical. In that case the norm would be provided by a philosophical and anthropological reflection on humanity, on what makes up the *humanum*, and then by the question of the specific reality in which this *humanum* can develop or be prevented from developing. Galatians 3.28 would be that kind of norm, formulated in terms of what makes up humanity, even if the reality does not match the claim. If historical research establishes what really happened, it cannot say anything about why it happened like this and why it needed to. If it nevertheless does so, it makes the actual findings the criterion of judgment and delivers itself over to the criticism of the facts, or goes beyond the competence of its methods.

11. But that which can be established factually and empirically and is accessible to experience cannot be normative in establishing what is also right and significant for human action. A position which refuses to adopt a critical detachment in thought and thus in action by referring to the immediacy of such experience sets one possible experience over against another possible experience. It is then possible to have an admirable argument at this level for evermore or to seek a protective shelter of communal emotional well-being with others who have had such experiences – two courses which can be demonstrated from the feminist literature and praxis of sisterhood. Moreover, these courses have also been taken in the controversies of male scientists and in the formation of male cliques. It follows from this that, quite apart from the man-woman problem, a science which follows the method of the individual sciences in looking for facts, whether in the sphere of

historical research, of sociology or psychology, does not solve the problems of the person who can motivate himself or herself against facts.

12. The solution does not lie in hostility to science but in the differentiation of scientific methods, also in respect of these limitations. Men oppress women – that is the result of many empirical investigations. But Ivan Illich, for example, does not attempt to clarify further why that is so.[14] He keeps to the empirical level, which he describes as the battlefield of the sexes. His solution provides adequate weapons for both sides, and not just for men, in the hope that this would lead to a cease-fire and that the balance of terror would provide the possibility of each side taking similar vengeance on the other in the case of a declaration of war.[15] In fact, if science were in principle identical with the discovery of empirical material, then men and women would remain victims of their socialization, their psychological determination, and the network of political and economic conditions of their time.

Any criticism of the 'omnipotence' of the empirical sciences is welcome, no matter from what quarter it comes. Today it often also comes from women. The limitations of the empirical model need to be shown, particularly in the scientific sphere. Reflections on human beings, on their capacity to motivate themselves, to become aware of the motives for their action, to ask about meaning, to govern themselves freely in the face of empirical experience, belong in the sphere of science, but a science which has taken a different 'subject' from the empirical one, namely human beings themselves as they think, decide and act, to the degree that they find and realize meaning.

So there is a need, which cannot be regarded as a task specific to either sex, to distinguish the different levels of reflection and the methods which are used, including the awareness of what can be done here to grasp the many-sidedness of human reality and conditioning.

13. I attempted to make distinctions of this kind in a series of lectures which I gave in the winter semester of 1984/85 in the Protestant Theological Faculty in Vienna, explaining them in connection with select and topical themes in feminine theology. In doing this I was concerned to give a critical survey of the

argument and positions of this theology with a view to distinguishing real results from the products of wishful thinking. I have
taken over this approach for the present study, which is to be in
two volumes, but have developed it further and added a systematic
chapter providing a basic criticism of the principles of feminist
theology, which is indispensable. In terms of method and theme
I have divided the material into two blocks, which in the two
volumes correspond to this basic criticism. 1. In this first volume,
Women and Early Christianity, I shall be concerned to provide a
methodological discussion of what historical research can and
cannot achieve. For this I have chosen themes which are relevant
within theology and which according to my varied experiences
over many years of lecturing are also keenly discussed outside the
university: the tradition(s) about Jesus, Pauline theology, the
controversy with Gnosticism and the evidence of the Pastoral
Epistles. Along with a few references, by way of example, to the
further development of these themes in the church fathers, the
result is a short history of early Christianity from the perspective
of its interest in women. 2. The second volume will be entitled
The Revival of the Goddesses. It will take for granted the use of
the historical method and use the Old Testament rejection of the
fertility cult and the hypotheses of the early matriarchies to raise
systematic questions about the sacralization of eros and questions
of myth and history. Here within a systematic theological reflection I shall be concerned with the God-Father/God-Mother question and the problem of analogy and about 'Jesa Christa' and the
problem of idealizing. I shall end by putting forward a view of a
'feminine science' as a new form of the old problem of the
relationship of theory to praxis.

14. The women's movement began with an outcry, an outcry
against the violation of basic human rights and an appeal for the
development and recognition of the living reality of the feminine
dimension of humanity. There were no sober reflections, considerations, differentiations behind this. Anyone not involved must
have found such an outcry irrational: aggressive, threatening and
even contemptuous of the humanity for which the women were
supposed to stand. The refusal to make woman responsible for
the *humanum* which was withheld from her seemed a sign of
revolution, and would continue to do so as long as this circle was

not broken. There was no room for distinctions at that point; they would have weakened a movement which was no longer concerned to negotiate, since negotiations could not bring it to its goal. The vehemence of irrational emotions must be accepted for this first phase of the women's movements. At a next stage this outcry began to take literary form in a fantasy of conversion: the solidarity of women, sisterhood, the reality of feminine life as a dominant theme at work in history. There was no longer any debate about the masculine reality of life, far less about a mediation between the two: the worlds were divided, as before, but this time the world of women was to stand in the foreground. The outcry was followed by a reversal of values in which the lowest were to become the highest. Where the outcry is interpreted as being irrational, the fantasy of conversion seems an illusion. But those involved often live more by illusions. Often that is the only way.

15. Much has changed in the meantime, not least thanks to the irrational and illusory characteristics of the women's movements. New laws anchor the equality of the sexes under the claim for justice. Women are coming into public view in politics and the academic world. Women are writing – and their books are being read. Women's projects are being encouraged by institutions, and are being financed. Most of the Reformed churches now accord women equal rights as ministers. And yet the eternal prejudices against women are still detectable. The law prevents actual discrimination, but does not affect human attitudes, those things which form the horizon of their motivations.[16] But it is precisely here that the prejudices are to be found. Law creates the necessary framework for action, but it does not provide the motivation, which would make the law superfluous if it were governed by the criterion of justice.

16. After the outcry and the fantasy of conversion, something else is now necessary: a struggle – which is going to be a hard one – with the reality principle; a reflection which dares to objectivize, even if it proves that what should be is not so nor ever was in history: argumentation as a weapon of reason against ideologies and prejudices; differentiation in the analysis on either side, male and female, with the help of methodological exactness – exactness, honesty, capacity for criticism, even if the other side takes this as

weakness and censures it as adaptation. No one gets anywhere without risks.

That is followed by a further step, towards an alliance of the sexes. Oppression, compulsion, writes Martin Buber, are a negative reality; they meant oppression and rebellion. But the opposite pole is not freedom, but alliance. 'Freedom is a possibility, possibility regained.' The feminist movement has done much to be proud of in connection with this freedom. But: 'The opposite to being constrained by destiny, by nature, by humanity is not being free from destiny, from nature, from humanity, but being involved and allied with it; for this to happen one must, of course, become independent, but this independence is a stage and not somewhere to live in.'[17]

Men and women can make war on one another or separate from one another, whether by genus-structure or sisterhood, but it is together that they make up the reality which is human life. Both sexes face the demand to preserve their humanity in life together. That, too, is a decisive contribution towards peace.

However clearly the history of failure in the relationship between the sexes can be demonstrated, the negative evidence of history must not be and remain the criterion. From humanity as a specific feature of the human race on the one hand and from belief in creation and redemption on the other it must be possible to counter prejudices through criticism, and negative experiences through active hope.

CHAPTER ONE

History Speaks with Two Tongues

Is Eve guilty of everything?

Human history is a history of crises, smouldering and escalating, hidden and open, individual and on a world-political scale. The Christian confession of faith connects the answer to the obvious question why that is so with the biblical story of the Fall in Genesis 3. With the Fall humanity loses the Garden of God and enters upon its history, in which it forfeits all that it had in the Garden of Eden. As a result human beings create their 'slaughterhouse', including the much-cited war between the sexes. People? No, Eve, the first woman was responsible for it all. Eve opposes the divine commandment, she succumbs to the whispering of the evil serpent, she gives man the fruit.

But why Eve and not Adam? The Old Testament scholar Hermann Gunkel gives the answer: 'The woman is more lively and covetous and awakens before the man.'[18] Gunkel finds this scene 'piquant' and a masterpiece of psychological description.[19] 'In an innocent and childlike way she longs for the most momentous act of her life', and it does not surprise Gunkel that Adam was more quickly motivated to eat the fruit by the snake than was Eve: 'If the woman leads him astray, the man cannot resist.'[20] The woman's longing for the man and the tyranny of the man over the woman are established from that point on. 'The woman desires her own slavery.'[21] The war between the sexes becomes an ingredient of human history.

The ongoing influence of this interpretation can be traced further into the Midrashim of the rabbinic tradition, the New Testament texts and beyond. A Gunkel-style argument is still current even among those whose thought and feelings are secular,

despite their ignorance of the Christian tradition: women are
more easily led astray and need the man's strong hand to keep
them in order.

There is a close connection between commonplaces of this kind
and the biblical creation stories. In the Pastoral Epistles, which
were not written by Paul, although they explicitly mention Paul
as their author,[22] the subordination of women is backed up with
two arguments: Adam was created first (I Tim.2.13 with a
reference to the second creation narrative in Gen.2) and 'Adam
was not deceived, but the woman was deceived and became a
transgressor' (I Tim.2.14). The unknown author of I Timothy
passes an even sharper judgment on Eve than the author of Gen.3:
Adam was not led astray at all, which means that Eve was guilty
of everything.

There is evidence that as the influence of the story continued,
the beginning of sin was increasingly blamed on Eve. In his
wisdom sayings Jesus Sirach (beginning of the second century BC),
deals with 'evil women as the worst thing there is and the good
fortune bestowed by a well-behaved wife'.[23] Who would deny
that there are 'evil' women just as there are also evil men? But the
reason given for women being evil again comes from a more
pointed interpretation of Gen.3: 'From a woman sin had its
beginning, and because of her we all die.'[24]

The extra-biblical book the Apocalypse of Moses, written
about the beginning of our era, tells the story of the life and death
of Adam and Eve. It includes the following episode. When Adam
fell ill at the age of 930 he called all his sons to him and told them
the story of the Garden of Eden to explain the reason for his
sickness: 'When God made us, me and your mother, through
whom I am dying...'[25] And Eve acknowledges: 'My lord Adam,
rise, give me half your illness and let me bear it, because this has
happened to you through me.'[26] This confession is repeated when
Eve's son Seth is attacked by a wild beast: 'Woe is me! For when
I come to the day of resurrection, all who have sinned will curse
me, saying that Eve did not keep the command of God.'[27] Eve
then admonishes the beast to stop its bad behaviour. The beast
replies: 'O Eve, neither your greed nor your weeping are due to
us, but to you, since the rule of the beasts has happened because
of you. How is it that your mouth was opened to eat from the tree

concerning which God commanded you not to eat from it? Through this also our nature was changed. Therefore now you would not bear it if I begin to reprove you.'[28] The beast listens to Seth himself, who then puts the same arguments to it, and slinks back into its den. Thus rebuked on all sides Eve finally falls to the ground and cries in desperation to God: 'I have sinned, O God; I have sinned, O Father of all; I have sinned against you, I have sinned against your chosen angels, I have sinned against the cherubim, I have sinned against your steadfast throne; I have sinned, Lord, I have sinned much, and all sin in creation has come about through me.'[29]

A second work of the same literary genre, the Life of Adam and Eve, written at the same time as the Apocalypse of Moses and identical to it in many passages, begins with the time after the expulsion from Paradise. Adam and Eve find nothing to eat and Eve immediately says that this is her fault: 'My Lord, would you kill me? O that I would die! Then perhaps the Lord God will bring you again into Paradise, for it is because of me that the Lord God is angry with you.'[30] Adam rejects this demand, as he will not lift up his hand against his own flesh. He resolves on an act of penitence so that God may again become gracious. Eve is to stand in the river Tigris for thirty-seven days and Adam in the water of the Jordan for forty. After eighteen days Satan becomes angry because he is afraid that this action may succeed. He changes into a figure of light, rushes to Eve in the Tigris and succeeds in leading her astray a second time by persuading her that God has forgiven her, and prepares to get food for her. Eve interrupts her work of penitence. When Adam sees them both coming he cries out with tears: 'O Eve, Eve, where is the work of your penitence? How have you again been seduced by our enemy?'[31] By contrast Adam persists, and Eve again asks to die: 'You live on, my lord. Life is granted to you, since you have done neither the first nor the second error, but I have been cheated and deceived, for I have not kept the command of God. And now separate me from the light of such life.'[32] Not only did Eve begin all the evil; through her it never finds an end.

In the second half of the second century Tertullian, the church father who is most quoted by the feminists, wrote a work against the adornment of women. He, too, talks about Eve:

No one of you all, best beloved sisters, from the time that she had... learned concerning her own (that is, woman's) condition, would have desired too gladsome (not to say too ostentatious) a style of dress; so as not rather to go about in humble garb, and rather to negelect her appearance, walking about as Eve mourning and repentant, in order that by every garb of penitence she might the more fully expiate that which she derives from Eve – the ignominy, I mean, of the first sin, and the odium attaching to her as the cause of human perdition. 'In pains and in anxieties you bear children, woman; and towards your husband is your inclination and he lords it over you.' Do you not know that you are each an Eve? The sentence of God on this sex of yours lives in this age: the guilt must of necessity live too. You are the devil's gateway: you are the unsealer of that forbidden tree: you are the first deserter of the divine law: you are she who persuaded him whom the devil was not valiant enough to attack. You destroyed so easily God's image, man. On account of your guilt... even the Son of God had to die. And do you think about adorning yourself over and above your tunics of skins?[33]

The biblical Eve is a representative of 'woman'. If we sum up what is said in the texts quoted, we get the following picture: 'woman' is the first and often the only one to bear the blame for the coming of sin and disaster into the world. Covetous and easily led astray, she constantly succumbs to temptation and is responsible for the continuation of the disaster. She brings death and herself has deserved death. Condemned by God and all creation she spends her life in subjection to man, in constant despair and penitence, including appropriate penitential garb. Despite what is said in Gen.1.27 she is excluded from being in the image of God and is in good company with the Jews, because indirectly she, too, has the death of the Son of God on her conscience.

However, this tradition, attested by texts, which has also found a way into the New Testament, contrasts with another which says that Adam is responsible for everything. In IV Ezra, an apocalyptic book, written towards the end of the first century,[34] the visionary speaks with God in order to understand the evil course of the world: 'And you led him (Adam) into the garden which your right hand had planted before the earth appeared. And you laid upon him one commandment of yours; but he transgressed it; and immediately you appointed death for him and for his descendants.'[35] But that had consequences for all humanity: 'For the first Adam, burdened with an evil heart, transgressed and was overcome, as were also all who were descended from him. Thus the disease became permanent.'[36] And God replied to Ezra: 'I made the world for their sake, and when Adam transgressed my statutes, what had been made was judged.'[37] Finally Ezra laments: 'O Adam, what have you done? For though it was you who sinned, the fall was not yours alone, but ours also who are your descendants.'[38]

The Syrian Apocalypse of Baruch, which is related to IV Ezra,[39] offers comparable statements about the guilt of Adam. Thus God says to the seer: 'For what did it profit Adam that he lived nine hundred and thirty years and transgressed that which he was commanded? Therefore, the multitude of time that he lived did not profit him, but it brought death and cut off the years of those who were born from him.'[40] 'For although Adam sinned first and has brought death upon all who were not in his own time, yet each of them who has been born from him has prepared for himself the coming torment.'[41] 'Adam is, therefore, not the cause, except only for himself.'[42] 'And as you first saw the black waters on top of the cloud which first came down upon the earth,' says the angel Ramiel, interpreting the terrifying vision of God's judgment on the world to Baruch, 'this is the transgression which Adam, the first man, committed. For when he transgressed, untimely death came into being... illness was created, labour accomplished... the realm of death began to ask to be renewed with blood, the conception of children came about, the passion of the parents was produced, the loftiness of men was humiliated.'[43]

These conceptions from apocalyptic underlie the so-called Adam-Christ typology of Paul in Romans (5.12-21). 'Therefore as sin came into the world through one man and death through sin and so death spread to all men....'[44] Through the transgression of Adam, Paul writes, damnation came upon humanity and death gained the mastery. Through the disobedience of the one the many were made sinners. Adam is the counterpart of the future humanity redeemed by Jesus Christ. The same idea occurs in I Cor.15.21,22,45.[45]

This tradition can also be pursued as far as the writings of the church fathers. In Chapter 14 of his *Enchiridion* Augustine refers to Paul and Romans: 'That one sin, admitted into a place where such perfect happiness reigned (Paradise), was of so heinous a character that by one man the whole race was originally, and as one may say, radically condemned; and it cannot be pardoned and blotted out except through the one mediator...'[46] Cyril, Bishop of Jerusalem from 351, i.e. three years before Augustine was born, writes in his baptismal catechesis: 'The sin of one man, Adam, could bring death to the world.'[47] As a third example it is worth quoting from John Chrysostom, who came from Antioch, and was also an approximate contemporary of the two church fathers already mentioned. As he puts it in the homilies on Genesis: 'For the tasting of its fruit (i.e. the fruit of the tree) and the transgression of the commandment brought death to Adam.'[48] Sin took its beginning through Adam. Adam had not tolerated the good life in Paradise, '... but transgressed the bounds of what he had been commanded by unspeakable frivolity'.[49]

Adam stands for 'humanity', and from these texts, too, it is possible to compile a 'horror picture' of the male, as we did earlier in the case of Eve. Nevertheless, we must grant both the Jewish and the Christian tradition that it is also possible to find sufficient texts that speak of the guilt of the first human couple, or of the guilt of both, 'humankind' or Satan.[50] It is also possible to collect the statements together in selective series under these perspectives.

Using methods

What is common to all the texts cited despite the different statements that they make? Their naive exegesis. For without doubt the text of Genesis 3 says that Eve was first led astray and then Adam. One can now give rein to one's associative imagination and say in the interest of feminists that Eve was bound to have been led astray by something as unusual as a talking serpent. Moreover the serpent had to make an effort and argue. And Eve had a laudable intention: she wanted to become wise. By contrast Adam let an ordinary woman bewitch him[51] and is to be numbered among those obtuse people who go along with what is suggested to them.[52]

But although they can add an amusing touch to some debates, such 'pious' fabrications remain caught up in that naive attitude which begins from a biblical text as it stands. In the meantime biblical scholarship has established a more sophisticated range of methods which is not to be looked down on as much as some feminists suppose.[53] If one looks at the tradition about Adam and Eve, the question arises who 'really' is responsible for the Fall and how the contradictions can be resolved.

Historical-critical work attempts to go one step 'behind' the texts and look for the social context in which they arose. Texts are composed by people who live in a society at a particular time in a particular situation and have particular problems which they attempt to solve.

Genesis 3 has an 'aetiological' character, and that means that the narrative is meant to explain an existing practice.[54] Here the historical experience which gives rise to the question why something is and is experienced is held to be the result of a cause lying outside history, in primeval times. Here is an example from Greek mythology: 'Because the goddess (Demeter) on arriving in Eleusis rejected the wine and drank *kykeion*, they drink *kykeion* at the festival at Eleusis... In reality they drank *kykeion* because this was the customary farmers' drink before the introduction of the vine.'[55] That the serpent is a threat to humanity, that pregnancy and birth bring burdens and pains on women, that women exercise a seductive erotic charm on men, that men tyrannize women, that women allow this and nevertheless 'run after' men, that work requires labour, that man must struggle to get his food from the earth and that death finally overshadows all things – all this is the bitter reality of the unparadisal existence of humanity. The question why that 'must' be is answered by the story of the Fall.

So the mythological parts of Genesis begin from experience, and through the *aition* bestow on it the character of something that is eternally valid. Therefore aetiologies are circular arguments: what is, must be as it is, and what must be, is so – a naive attempt at explaining reality of a kind that we can no longer make in the same way. However, a theological statement that is handed down with the mythological narrative of Genesis 3 remains important: the fact that men dominate women is the consequence of a disruption, a situation which goes against God's good will for creation.

If we investigate the historical context of the text further we find ourselves at the time of the hey-day of the monarchy in Israel.[56] The author, of whom we have no knowledge as a person, is writing at a time when Israel had already conquered the so-called land of Canaan[57] and had settled there. Its relationship to the original inhabitants of the land, who had largely remained neighbours, seems to have been extremely ambivalent. On the one hand the faith of Israel was in the sharpest contradiction to the religion of the Canaanites, and this strand of the tradition remained dominant. On the other hand there were a great many processes of assimilation, reinterpretation and new interpretations as a result of the political, social and cultural environment. Evidence for this is not least the monarchy in Israel 'as is the custom among all the peoples' (I Sam.8.5). Canaanite religion, itself shaped by Egyptian influences and Aegean culture,[58] had influential goddesses in its pantheon who played an important role in the cosmogonies as 'bearers of the gods' and the world. This traditional material is known to the author of Genesis 3, though the ideas with which he works cannot be reconstructed in detail. Nevertheless it is striking that he takes up themes from archaic myths and puts them in a negative form. Thus it is said, for example, of the goddess Eurynome that she was at the beginning, that she creates divine nature, e.g. the serpent Ophion, couples with it, and in the form of a dove lays the world egg from which there emerges everything that makes up the world: sun, moon, stars, earth, rivers, plants and living beings.[59] In Genesis 3, also, Eve is the main figure, though she is not a goddess, for that would go against the faith of Israel. Adam is mentioned only in a subordinate clause, for Eve's counterpart is the serpent, which speaks and knows of divine mysteries – in other words has a divine character. The two do not couple, but their common action has a decisive result: the 'new' world of sin and death. Parallel themes can be recognized, but they have clearly been turned into their opposite.

The historical and political context of this text, Israel in the first phase of the monarchy, was characterized by the battle of the prophetic tradition against the religion of Canaan, which was always also political. This battle also included criticism of a monarchy which right from the occasion of its origin tended towards assimilation to the Canaanite cultural environment, even though this assimilation did not come about to any great extent. In this connection the royal harem plays a role as early as the time of King David, and even more so in that of Solomon, who did not restrict himself to 'indigenous' women. But the queens of Israel brought with them the religious cults with which they were familiar, so that Yahweh, the God of Israel, became one among many gods and indeed goddesses. The prophetic history-writing sees this apostasy to the alien idols as the occasion for punitive judgment by Yahweh, which finally leads to the destruction of the kingdom and the dispersion of the people.[60] Thus Genesis 3 and Eve make Solomon's 'wicked wives' into wicked women generally[61] and we again have an aetiology. This time it refers not only to general human experiences but also to a particular political situation.

A superficial demythologization which keeps to eliminating the talking serpent from the text because we all know that serpents cannot speak remains at as naive a level as a form of exegesis which says 'That's what's in the text.' And in understanding and resolving the contradictory chains of tradition from which we began the question of the author and his historical situation is decisive, since from that one can discover the interest which gives a text its form. Genesis 3 was written from the perspective of a man living in the first millennium BC under the rule of David and Solomon in Israel, in particular political and social conditions, with the problems and questions to which they gave rise. So what the text says must be read in the light of a particular historical situation and from the perspective of the author.

So historical criticism can show the circumstances in which texts come into being. This view, which demythologizes the claim of eternal validity, has come into being in our tradition not by chance, but in opposition to the naive understanding which has derived unconditional statements for faith from historical circumstances. Therefore not only science should have an interest in submitting itself to the strictness of such an analysis.

A next methodological stage is linked to the concept of interest:

hermeneutics. Texts are written by human beings, human beings are shaped by the realities in which they live, so individuals or groups are the filter through which every tradition goes. Not only are these historical circumstances normative for a text but also the attitude, the view, the judgment of those who prove responsible for it. The interest which governs an author is also determined by the group which he is addressing. When, for example, in the writing I have already quoted, Tertullian rages on about the adornment of women – an interest which he shares with some feminists who rightly condemn fashion as an unworthy way of catching men and luxury as a privilege of the ruling class – he can hardly quote Adam as biblical legitimation.[62] The realities of life and preunderstanding as determining influences on the one hand and opinion, judgment, attitude, as the way in which people react to what they experience on the other hand, form the particular principle of selection. Therefore the author's biography and personality are decisive in interpreting his remarks. Anyone who selects, as it were cuts swathes through the luxuriant vegetation of existing traditional material. Some speak of Eve, others of Adam; what superficially seems like a contradiction emerges on closer inspection to be different kinds of interest.

The barrier of contradictions

Feminists pounce with great verve on the contradictions within the Christian tradition (nor are they the only ones to do so). But they themselves are also subject to the hermeneutical principle of interest and selection. Some, above all on the radical wing, combine with it an interest in disqualifying Christianity and declaring it to be obsolete.[63] Something that contains so many contradictions cannot lay any claim to the truth. Others select and form negative chains. Everything Christian from Genesis 3 to the present discrimination against women in the churches – above all in the Roman Catholic Church – seems to them to be patriarchalist terror. Yet others select in positive chains and with much labour bring to light the overgrown salvation history of women which is understand to belong to the basic ingredients of the Christian confession.[64]

In this way the chain of contradictions also continues in the church. Which verdict is right in the case of Christianity versus women? Who is right, the Apocalypse of Moses or IV Ezra? The author of I Timothy or Paul? Tertullian or John Chrysostom? Mary Daly or Elisabeth Moltmann-Wendel? These contradictions can only be worked through and resolved if we put the question in another way. What interests do the Apocalypse of Moses, Paul, Tertullian, Mary Daly have?

Radical feminists like Mary Daly call for 'Methodicide'. The methods of male scholars are, they say, an instrument for the oppression of women because they kill creative thought, argue in a circle and function as a fetish: scientific methods as sets of distorting mirrors are simply the mechanisms of male needs for domination.[65] Over against that I would set the demand for even more precise methods, for the application of more, and more varied, methods, in order to examine the problem closely from as many sides as possible, for still greater objectivity which seeks to do justice to the alien and the unfamiliar, even if this goes against one's own attitude. Only then is it possible to occupy an independent position, to some degree independent of ideological interests, which agrees with a tradition or differs from it for good reasons.

All the scientific methods that have been developed or taken over in the sphere of theology, particularly since the Enlightenment, have a critical, demythologizing, emancipatory stamp which acts in the interest of women. Mary Daly also points that out in her first 1968[66] book: what is now rejected by scientific knowledge was for centuries 'slipped in'.[67] Even worse, what is rejected by scientific knowledge is even now being proclaimed in an obstinate way from pulpits and cathedras as the word of God. The ominous statement, 'believing does not mean knowing', still seems to possess its stubborn validity.

Here a new and ominous contradiction opens up, namely that between scientific reflection and communication. Believing Christians still find that what for a biblical scholar is daily bread is a trial to them, because as a rule in school and church they are presented only with the naive exegesis of, say, a Tertullian (and with things that are even more naive), the effect of which has such disastrous consequences for women. Two barriers stand in the way of honest communication even today: the formation of an academic élite and the teaching authority of the church (especially in the Roman Catholic Church).

Let me list briefly the reasons for this: from the perspective of the sociology of knowledge it can be demonstrated that knowledge is always a power factor. Being in possession of knowledge thus leads to the formation of an élite. Thus for example the interest of institutions of education is also divided: on the one hand they want to make knowledge accessible to everyone on the basis of equality of opportunities; on the other they represent a harsh apparatus of selection which excludes more people than it encourages. Here knowledge becomes the criterion of selection, the hurdle which decides on a person's later place in society. There are fewer good places than bad, and these few places are defended. Anyone who ultimately wants to belong to the élite must survive a whole series of hard tests, and not everyone has the necessary persistence. There is no question that in this connection knowledge can be used for male, and not only male, needs for domination. But the significance of knowledge cannot be defined only in the light of this function. That would be too simplistic.[68]

Quite independently of the role of knowledge as a selection principle, wanting to know is an effort. The resistance put up by history to the researcher is great: looking for sources, learning languages, getting an overall view, collecting, comparing, putting forward hypotheses, verifying, falsifying and beginning all over again; recognizing formal structures through the wealth of material, looking through and judging motives for action without reading one's own into them so that the whole thing does not turn into a conversation with oneself. All that takes time, energy, asceticism, which not everyone is willing and able to devote to it. It is not just a matter of power.

Human reality, which underlies every tradition, is complex, more complex than our awareness and its capacity to grasp it. It is no coincidence that people tend to generalize, to simplify, to form pre-judgments (to begin with still in a neutral sense). Certainty is created only by that which constantly recurs;[69] there is a clear likelihood of continually seeing the familiar where it cannot be found. Losing certainties or having them destroyed makes people anxious. Belonging to a group is indicated by fixed opinions; who likes standing alone, who can live in the long term only by causing provocation? So the desire for a murder of methods is understandable and at the same time a sign of belonging to the feminist camp.

Nevertheless I would maintain the significance of scientific method and theorizing: a supply of knowledge rather than an attitude of knowing; differentiation and accurate analysis rather than simplification; responsibility rather than stultification; letting oneself be asked questions rather than prejudice; the attempt to understand rather than exploiting contradictions; the question of meaning rather than the fullness of possible experience. Only on this presupposition will it be possible to deal with the disparate elements of tradition. The fact that Christianity is contradictory in its attitude towards women has meanwhile become a commonplace in more than feminist literature. It is the merit of feminist interest that here it has not at all been concerned with superficial attempts at harmonization. It has put its finger on a problem of which many Christian women have not been aware, but which was and is detectable and can be put like this: where is my place between Eve and Mary, heroine and servant, saint and whore? In the biblical texts and also in subsequent tradition it is possible to find relevant texts for each position and there is nothing more paralysing than conversations between feminists and anti-feminists in which biblical quotations and texts from the church fathers are hurled from side to side. In the best of cases the battle lines remain, even if they do not harden further.

However, contradictions are not just the result of patriarchal or other such deliberate malice. How can they come into existence?

First, difference of place and time in history plays a part. That was already clear from Genesis 3 and the circumstances in which this text came into being. Secondly, there is the difference in states of awareness at a particular time. Knowledge, too, is subject to a process of development in which there is regress as well as progress. One cannot accuse say Tertullian of a lack of historical-critical reflection, but one can make that criticism of a preacher who has qualified in theology. Thirdly, people have different attitudes and therefore interests. They can be more or less free in respect of their historical conditioning. The theoretical human capacity for self-determination in freedom provides a capacity for resistance, for outlining new things, for opposition to the ordinary.

Whether this capacity is realized remains a personal matter. Fourthly, different interests and accordingly different arguments provoke different dimensions of one and the same person. Fifthly, note must be taken of the distance between the place where a text comes into being and the place where it is received. A reader's own interest easily misleads him or her into reading something out of or into a text which on close inspection cannot be justified in terms of the author's intent. Sixthly, one's own self-critical experience should make one aware that there are contradictions in human beings themselves which cannot immediately be resolved. At the level of the unconscious as discovered by psycho-analysis contradictions intensify and here the question of the unconscious introduces more problems than solutions outside therapeutic dialogue.[70] Seventhly, the nature of a text, its literary genre, must be noted. Contradictions arise when, for example, allegories or myths are taken literally, ethical demands and statements of experience are not distinguished. Eighthly, many contradictions may be explained in terms of the difference between claim and reality, ethical demand and refusal or failure, which cannot be overcome in principle. And ninthly, as 'citizens of two worlds' (Kant) human beings are in irresolvable tension between animality and reason, nature and spirit, objectivity and being an 'I', compulsion and freedom, immediacy and reflection – and this tension which is experienced as contradiction. Though we are aware that we can be human beings only in a totality, nevertheless separation is catching us up. This opposition in experience is confirmed precisely through the demand for a whole life which is constantly expressed, especially in feminist literature. Being whole is not something given to human beings; it is a task for them to achieve.

The example of Tertullian

In this section I want to give specific examples of these nine at present abstract principles from the Christian tradition. Here I am deliberately beginning from a desire to understand what seems contradictory before passing judgment on it.

Tertullian constantly provokes the most vehement and spon-taneous defensive reaction in feminist circles. So I find it attractive to choose him in particular in order to examine possibilities of understanding. In his second letter to his own wife, the very Tertullian who admonishes all women to dress as Eve in penitence, since Eve alone was responsible for sin and death coming into the world, adopts other tones. He ends with praise of Christian marriage: 'Both are brother and sister, both fellow servants, no difference of spirit or of flesh; they are truly two in one flesh. Where the flesh is one, the spirit also is one. Together they pray, together prostrate themselves, together perform their fasts; mutually teaching, mutually exhorting, mutually sustaining. They are equally both found in the church of God; equally at the banquet of God; equally in straits, in persecutions, in refreshments.'[71] However, he ends his treatise against the adornment of women with the following words: '...implanting in your ears the word of God; fitting on your necks the yoke of Christ! Submit your head to your husbands, and you will be enough adorned. Busy your hands with spinning; keep your feet at home; and you will please better than by arraying yourselves in gold.'[72]

In the second passage he talks of being subject to husbands, in the first he talks of husband and wife as brother and sister; in the second he talks of house and housework, in the first of common worship and says that one does not have an advantage over another. The suggestion that Tertullian thinks that women could be less steadfast in persecution because they are so easily misled is not confirmed.

Different audiences lead to different kinds of arguments. It is understandable that Tertullian repudiates women who think mainly of cosmetics, dress and hair-style; but that does not mean that he looks at all women in this way. He talks to his wife differently. But if one goes on to consider the interest that motivates him in the letters to his wife, a new theme emerges: Tertullian does not want his wife to marry a second time, perhaps a Gentile, should he die earlier than she. Therefore he stresses Christian marriage as a special form of the relationship between husband and wife.

It is not least because Tertullian, the educated lawyer, was already married when he became a Christian, that he has nothing against marriage: 'We do not indeed forbid the union of man and woman, blessed by God as the seminary of the human race, and devised for the replenishment of the earth and the furnishing of the world.'[73] But he knows Paul's proviso in I Corinthians (7.9); the apostle, 'indeed permits marrying, but prefers abstinence; the former on account of the insidiousnesses of temptations, the latter on account of the straits of the times. Now by looking into the reason thus given for each proposition, it is easily discerned that the ground on which the power of marrying is conceded is necessity; but whatever necessity grants she by her very nature depreciates. In fact, in that it is written "To marry is better than to burn", what is the nature of this "good" which is only commended by comparison with "evil"? How much better is it neither to marry nor to burn.'[74] There follows a comparison: marriage is like flight from persecution – life without marriage is like honest confession and a martyr's death.

Now at all events Tertullian lived in accordance with the conviction he expressed in words: being ascetic in Paul's sense, which means remaining married in Christian responsibility, but not seeking marriage if one of the couple dies. The time and place in which he lived make some of that understandable. In constant waves of brutal persecution Christians were faced with the irresolvable alternatives: death or denial of their Christian identity.[75] Such a demand is more existential than the question whether or not to marry. Moreover in the Jewish-Christian tradition marriage is bound up with having children, who in those conditions would simply face a cruel and early end.[76]

Against the background of the experience of persecution, torture and death the writing on female adornment also takes on new aspects: 'But Christians always, and now more than ever, pass their times not in gold but in iron: the stoles of martyrdom are now preparing... Do you go forth already arrayed in the cosmetics and ornaments of prophets and apostles.'[77] So adornment is contrasted with the prophetic and apostolic task. That Tertullian has no objection to prophetesses is also demonstrated by his later 'conversion' to the Gnostic group[78] of Montanists which in addition to its leader Montanus also had two prophetesses, Maximilla and Priscilla, in leading positions.

However, by themselves the persecutions of Christians would be too superficial an argument to make Tertullian's attitude comprehensible. He may have practised naive exegesis, but in his judgment and attitude to the world in which he lived, the Roman empire at the end of the second and the beginning of the third century, he was far from naive. Tertullian is evidence that the charges laid against the Christians of their time by their educated pagan opponents of hostility to the state, destructive refusal, opposition to the emperor, and betrayal of the ancient ideals of strength and value,[79] were correct.[80] But he and the Christians were not the only critics of the system.[81] Roman power politics did not favour individuals. The emperors attempted to keep themselves in power – but in vain – by wars which they deliberately started to keep the state treasury full and their soldiers occupied. Augustine, albeit two centuries later, compares the empire with a band of robbers.[82] Weary of the battles for power, even many decades before Tertullian's time shrewd statesmen sought peace and quiet in the country.[83] Politics was dominated by weariness at holding office. Rome's 'permissive patience',[84] a decisive ingredient of power politics, was rightly thought not to be a strength but a moral and religious weakness. City culture and luxury were increasingly regarded as 'silly artifices',[85] accompanied by anxiety over loss, the Roman anxiety about poverty.[86]

Not only was there open revolt against Rome, starting above all from the great cities, not least Jerusalem – at that time the Romans were still strong enough in military terms and in organization. The battle was carried on more subtly and more effectively: retreat into inwardness, into one's own world remote from the cruel business of politics; voluntary renunciation and the ideal of poverty, a renunciation of demonstrative pomp; a desire for redemption and apocalyptic fantasies of the imminent end of such a world in the awareness of not being one of the rejected. This refusal emanated from the philosophical and religious trends: Stoics, Cynics, mystics and – Christians.[87]

Tertullian is a radical opponent of the polytheistic régime. He sets against it the only God who stands above all the lords of the world as a just judge. Tertullian comes forward in his name. The symbol for that is the pallium, the simple mantle of the philosopher which he wears instead of the toga. In a writing on it he lets the pallium speak for itself: ' "I," it says, "owe no duty to the forum, the election-ground or the senate house; I keep no obsequious vigil, preoccupy no platforms, hover about no praetorian residences... I am no constant wearer out of benches, no wholesale router of laws, no barking pleader, no judge, no soldier, no king. I have withdrawn from the populace.'[88] Anyone who has nothing need not care for anything. That is the slogan of the church father who through quotation by the feminists has falsely gained the reputation of being an arch conservative.

Anyone who reads Tertullian can hardly escape the impression of direct parallels to the present in experience and judgment.[89] In his writing on the soul he depicts the world of his day: cultivated, civilized, everything is worked out and discovered, not a speck of dust is removed from human intervention. But: 'Our wants grow more and more keen, and our complaints more bitter in all mouths, whilst nature fails in affording us her usual sustenance.'[90] Tertullian storms against the frenzy of the mob at the theatre, against the idolatry of rank and office, against an ideal of honour which takes upon itself voluntary self-chastisement, torture and death.[91] And so he writes in his work on feminine adornment which has already been quoted many times: 'You ought to hate what ruined your fathers.'[92]

This also puts Tertullian's attitude towards women in a new light. He notes and prizes one who has the same Christian convictions as himself: he admonishes and makes demands on her. Otherwise women do not interest this radical ascetic and political subversive. The eschatological mood gives him no more joy than Paul before him at a world in which people marry and set up house and bring up children. 'Are we sure enough of our salvation that we have leisure for children?' And he continues somewhat cynically: 'Do we seek burdens for ourselves which are avoided even by the majority of the Gentiles, who are compelled by laws, who are decimated by abortions; burdens which finally are most of all unsuitable to us, as being perilous to faith?'[93] For children are ties to the 'bourgeois world'; they prevent renunciation and the ideal of poverty and being able to contemplate with tranquillity the end of this corrupt world. That children are the long chain by which women are above all bound is something of which feminists are also aware, and they express the fact without being deceived by romanticisms. Even if the occasion and motives are different, an understanding with Tertullian on this point would not be impossible. Tertullian has nothing against female prophets and apostles; on the contrary, if he had, he would not have turned to the Montanists. And another structural parallel emerges: Tertullian is just as radical and as hostile to scientific rationality and method as Mary Daly.[94] Even Tertullian's asceticism can be related to the withdrawal of women into sisterhood.

CHAPTER TWO

The Feminist Interest

Perspectives on Clement of Alexandria

While Tertullian is clearly rejected in feminist literature, opinion is divided over another church father, Clement of Alexandria. Mary Daly quotes him, like all the rest, as a deterrent,[95] Elaine Pagels puts positive stress on him as being well disposed towards women.[96] Clement of Alexandria became famous above all as a result of the catechetical school in Alexandria, at which he was a teacher at the end of the first and beginning of the second centuries. As a philosopher and theologian he is a systematic thinker who wants to talk to an educated audience or to educate his audience. For him, knowledge is the consummation of faith and faith the consummation of knowledge. Philosophy and theology, thought and faith do not contradict one another; rising from philosophical knowledge, with proper education, human beings can arrive at the ultimate knowledge of faith and perfection. Such a person is illuminated, the true 'Gnostic', elegant and attentive to the world. For Clement, a statement attributed to Tertullian, *credo quia absurdum*,[97] would be quite unthinkable. Elaine Pagels refers to the way in which he was shaped by the 'cosmopolitan atmosphere of Alexandria',[98] which, rich and educated, practised a different approach to women from that, say, of Tertullian.

Clement is indeed a man of moderation, who is able to give an impressive description of the dangers of passion, but he is no ascetic. He commends marriage 'for our country's sake and for the succession of children',[99] and also for bodily ailments, since the caring wife looks after husband, children and aged parents.[100] To emphasize that, he quotes the New Testament and refers to Matt.5.32: scripture counsels marriage. And as to behaviour in situations of persecution, scripture counsels flight as long as that is possible.[101]

In his comments on Clement's *Paidagogos* (The Instructor), the editor of a German volume of selections, Heinrich Kanz, says of Clement: 'The total equality of husband and wife could hardly be expressed more strongly...'[102] Here he is commenting on the following text: 'Let us, then, embracing more and more this good obedience, give ourselves to the Lord, clinging to what is surest, the cable of faith in him, and understanding that the virtue of woman and man is the same. For if the God of both is one, the master of both is also one: one church, one temperance, one modesty; their food is common, marriage an equal yoke; respiration, sight, hearing, knowledge, hope, obedience, love all alike. And those whose life is common, have common graces and a common salvation; common to them are love and training. Common, therefore, too, to men and women is the name of man.'[103]

Clement already does to a considerable degree what is called for today in feminist literature, namely to talk of God as a mother or in terms of motherhood: 'For when we were reborn in Christ, the one who gave birth to us again fed us with his own milk, the word; for it is appropriate that the being who bore us should immediately give his children food.'[104] Clement speaks of the tender and loving Father in heaven who lets his Word (Logos) trickle down as spiritual food: he speaks of those who flee to the reassuring breast of the Father, and praises them because they suckle this breast. That was one side of Clement of Alexandria; the other soon damps down all budding sympathy. Certainly for him man and woman are identical as far as virtue is concerned, but not when it comes to their nature. The male sex is therefore called to a higher capacity of knowledge than the female: 'Thus woman and man, free and slave, should be equally concerned for morality and justice and any other virtue, since it is a fit consequence that the same nature possesses one and the same virtue. We do not say that woman's nature is the same as man's as she is woman. As then there is sameness as far as respects the soul, woman will attain to the same virtue. But as there is a difference as regards the peculiar construction of the body (he means pregnancy and child-bearing), she is destined for child-bearing and housekeeping.'[105] And he continues: 'We do not train our women like Amazons to manliness in war; since we wish the men even to be peacable.'[106] Then follows a discourse on tribes with warlike women which ends: 'Women are therefore to philosophize equally with men, though the males are preferable at everything, unless they have become effeminate.'[107]

When specifically applied to the question of training the body this model works out as follows: 'Nor are women to be deprived of bodily exercise', and that means that they should 'exercise themselves in spinning, and weaving and superintending the cooks if necessary...'[108] Women are to get what is needed out of the provision store, tread the mill, do the cooking so that it tastes good to the husband, make the bed, get the drinks 'and so give exercise tending to good health...'[109] Women are to bathe for purification and for their health, men only for their health.[110] Women are to have children so that the city and the inhabited world do not go under for want of men.[111] This is the harmonious world of a 'bourgeois' idyll which Clement produces.

If we compare Tertullian and Clement, we find that more separates them than unites them: the one is ascetic, rigorous, separatist, and cares nothing for 'settled' family life with a house, children and possessions; he regards philosophy as arrogance and women as worth noting only when they take the radical way of faith, but then they may also perform spiritual functions. The other affirms the world, and is a mediator and a progressive thinker, who praises the family: he regards philosophy as the right way to the knowledge of God and women as being by nature destined to have a house and children.[112] The feminist estimation of these two prefers Clement, though his position represents the variant which is more harmful to the feminist interest. In respect of his attitude to women Tertullian argues from the claim of faith: but that is the more 'humane' version over against arguments in the light of nature, because in contrast to nature, faith is subject to decision. As has already been shown,[113] the theme of philosophy is a basic contradiction in human existence, between nature and spirit. The philosopher Clement is at home in this tradition and he 'resolves' the contradiction by attributing more nature to the female sex and more spirit to the male, in accordance with the usual 'division of work'.

The various perspectives in which Clement can be seen increase the range of contradictions in feminist literature. We should note that historical reality is complex, and that a comprehensive overall view, taking all motives and facts into account, is hardly possible.[114] There are contradictory strands of tradition, contradictions within a tradition or even a person, contradictions in reception and analysis. Anyone who cuts swathes determined by his or her own interest will always find enough points of contact to endorse that interest. History is either a chamber of horrors or a *camera caritatis*, depending on how one looks at it. Thus history always proves everything and there is no question of its independence.

Thus on closer analysis and with sufficient objectivity, and in this case also readiness to allow oneself to be alienated, many judgments cannot be justified, but on the contrary much that is strange can be understood. More exact knowledge of the actual circumstances in which an author lived and of his personality make many things plausible and capable of being understood; much can be explained from connections and dependent relationships in such a way that the contradictions are resolved. In this way justice is also done to history. However, it is at the price of one's own interest, which throws us back into the present.[115] And it is precisely there that one can find the significance of an exact consideration of history and becoming detached from oneself, in other words the significance of historical-critical work, namely recognizing that history does not legitimate our present interest and our options, but it cannot reject them as illegitimate either.[116] The feminist reading of the tradition attempts to form chains of legitimation in the same way as does the patriarchal reading. The history selected in this way justifies both. Statement stands over against statement, and each side regards its interest as a historical fact.

Where feminists make use of this method of selection and legitimation, contrary to their own desires[117] they discover no new methods; they make use of those of their opponents. Anyone who enjoys doing that may contrast the arguments of one series of selections with those of another. The fact remains that the counter-argument cannot be given, but that one interest comes up against its opposite. This stalemate can only be resolved when history is allowed an interest of its own through exact analysis and distancing and thus one's own interest is evident as such.

In specific terms that means that if a survey of the material in the tradition shows that since human thought began women have been regarded as a 'second sex',[118] there is still no justification here in maintaining and continuing the interest behind this state of affairs. Anyone who wants to attest and 'prove' his or her interest through history as something which is valid once and for all is involved in legitimation. But that also applies to the feminist side. So it is not a matter of opposing a feminist legitimation to a patriarchal legitimation but of criticizing the 'method' of legitimation itself. Where feminists refuse in principle to reflect on methods, as a logical consequence – *quod erat demonstrandum* – they can also conflict with women who, although beginning with the same interest, form other chains of legitimation. So as a first step I would argue that we should make use of neither the patriarchal reading nor the feminist reading, but of the exact reading which is in accordance with texts and authors. In that case it follows, for example, that Genesis 3 can be understood in terms of the time when the text was written, but is no longer totally valid for today; that Tertullian wants to live ascetically, but that not all individuals, women, share this life form, so that the problems of Tertullian are not their own; that Clement appeals to a philosophy which has developed further, specifically in view of the concept of nature, and today faces new and different problems.

Thus what is being discussed is not a new, feminist method but a new interest. So it will be necessary as a second stage to go on to ask what interest this is.

Interest and its effect

For someone to be occupied in doing something presupposes interest. Pupils do not learn without being interested. Any activity, whether intellectual or manual, is fed by interests. 'Interest in this sense is the complex of relevant motivations which govern the selectivity of my awareness.'[119] Psychology calls such relevant motivations 'attitudes';[120] the Vienna philosopher Erich Heintel speaks of the 'horizon of motivation' as the 'sphere of historically disclosed possibilities of action in which we can and must move and prove ourselves'.[121]

Interest can arise in three ways: it arises out of what I 'know', from 'the store of knowledge which is to hand,'[122] the 'habitual possession of my store of knowledge',[123] which does not represent any homogenous picture but extends 'from sure conviction through all shades of meaning including blind faith and indifference...'[124] Knowing here means more than just a clear insight which can be formulated; at the same time even what is unclear has relevance for motivation and can determine interest or all forms of activity.[125] An interest of this nature is aroused when the expectation of what is familiar is confirmed. This kind of interest can be described in terms of the positive significance of the concept of certainty and that of routine, which runs from being at least ambivalent to being negative. New, unknown, alien things are then rejected because they arouse no interest. However, it would be wrong to describe someone with this attitude as being without interest. His or her interest relates to what is familiar and not to asking questions. Indeed, even where people receive their tradition, one can begin from the fact that they tend to accept 'a congruence of experiences rather than the opposite'.[126] These considerations make it plausible why eisegesis (rather than exegesis), in other words reading one's own attitude into the texts of the tradition, is more popular than the attitude of allowing oneself to be alienated and 'disappointed'.

Now it may come about that because a new experience is alien, it may present a strong challenge, or a person – for whatever reasons in his or her personal history – may develop a greater degree of openness to new experience. This kind of interest thrives on the relationshiip of the familiar to the alien.[127] It is directed towards coping with a challenge to the existing store of knowledge, 'in order to investigate the atypical alien event which has proved to be "not like that but different"'.[128] In the course of appropriating the new, the existing store of knowledge changes. A third form of interest can arise from what Alfred Schütz calls 'imposed relevances'.[129] These play a role in educational institutions and their form of handing on knowledge, where interest is deliberately aroused. As we are not concerned with any educational themes, I shall leave this kind of interest out of account.

Feminist interest defines itself as being hostile to theory. Taking up the comments on the nature of interest described all too briefly above, in terms of the sociology of knowledge we must distinugish different types of theory-forming. Feminist criticism of theory is directed against the view that theory arises, as Karl Mannheim says, 'when someone thinks a system through to the end, works out some kinds of thought',[130] and in so doing refers to supra-temporal, extra-historical axioms, so that his statements take on the character of a truth 'in itself' and valid once and for all. Behind this is the idea of the 'autonomy of the theoretical sphere' over against historical conditions.[131] For feminists, such a theoretical understanding then arises, for example, in the axiom of the natural superiority of the male as a spiritual being or in the axiom that freedom from self-interest is necessary and possible in the service of the ideal of objectivity. So women contrast their subjective interest to the objective theory of male thought, feel themselves on the one hand subjected because their interests are not taken into account and on the other hand superior because they are confident enough to attack with their interests theory which takes no account of those interests.

Now this contrast is obsolete nowadays, since feminist interests, evidently without being aware of the fact, find themselves in the best company with the sociologists of knowledge at the beginning of our century (the history of their influence in Europe was interrupted or even broken off by the barbarity of the National Socialist régime). If anything becomes a problem to science, in other words to theory, then, as Karl Mannheim, whom I have already quoted, aptly puts it, it has already been a problem before in life. 'New forms of knowledge, in the last analysis, grow out of the conditions of collective life and do not depend for their emergence upon the prior demonstration by a theory of knowledge that they are possible; they do not therefore need to be first legitimized by an epistemology.'[132] Practical, extra-theoretical interest is the motivation and starting-point for processes of knowledge.

Feminist interest goes in two directions: finding an identity of the self and thus the person in his or her subjectivity, and being able to locate oneself in tradition as the objective side of reality. Both processes are related, and are the task of anyone who would and should find himself or herself in his or her history. What Karl Mannheim says about Ernst Troeltsch can be said *mutatis mutandis* of feminists who challenge theory which has already been characterized and is distinct from real life: 'But he no longer wants the withdrawn ivory tower of a type of scholar who, detached from life, unpolitical, inactive, investigates his specific problems in the apparent order of a mature world and leads his partial life. He seeks to stand in the midst of it and combine the lines of his theoretical interest with the suffering of a tumultuous world.'[133] *Mutatis mutandis* this means not only that one would have to replace the ivory tower of scholarly existence with the ivory tower of a housewife's existence but also that the feminist position, at any rate in its popularized forms, even wants to do away with lines of theoretical interest. But would that be at all possible?

If we begin from the insight of historicism in terms of the philosophy of history, a view which cannot accept either a religious order of life or a supra-historical and extra-historical ordering of the circumstances in which we live, it follows 'that knowledge of history becomes possible only from a fixable intellectual position, from a subject who wants the future and actively strives towards it.'[134] As subjects we select tradition, in order to be able to settle in it to serve our interest. But selection is a first step towards theory-forming, because we take some aspects and ignore other possible ones. We could not fully grasp the complex abundance of reality as a whole, nor would we want to without a selective interest. It is a fact 'that every theoretical and also every practical form of behaviour is selective'.[135] But this form of behaviour must be conscious, so that it is possible to deal responsibly with it.

It follows from this that neither women nor men, nor any human beings, can be blamed for a selective way of proceeding which only uses parts of reality, whether present or past. That way of proceeding is governed by the limitations of the human comprehension of reality. Therefore no judgment can be passed, either, as to whether one chain of selection is true or false in comparison with others: they are perspectivistic viewpoints conditioned by a person's position. This stage of theoretical reflection is important, for interest cannot and may not be held to be an objectively valid truth – that would mean legitimizing selection – , and what goes for objectively valid truth, e.g. as a so-called assured result of scholarship, is never without a degree of self-interest, even where this is concealed. The controversy between feminist and partriarchal historiography must be carried on at this level of differing interests and not intellectualized at the level of interest against.

What I have just said applies particularly when one is concerned with human beings in their history or their historicity, but not to the natural sciences, although a history of the development of the natural sciences can be written. However, that is of no interest in this context. Now if interest in reflecting on how we find access to our history is accepted, history must also constantly be rewritten, 'not in the sense of a correction but in the sense of a new overall orientation, which draws its principles, perspectives and criteria from a particular synthesis of the present'.[136] This does not completely destroy or merely supplement the other perspectives, but 'reorganizes' them from 'constantly new centres'.[137]

'Now these new centres have a basis beyond philosophy and beyond theory' (it would be less misleading had this statement spoken of 'before philosophy and before theory', so as not to produce the idea of something outside history) 'and depend on the new situation to which even the form of science belongs in a scientific age. In this sense they express the truth of the age in question.'[138] Feminist interest represents such a truth of our age, which first of all can be explained in terms of nothing but the interest which is manifest and as such undeniable.

The return of the vanished women

The feminist reading of the Christian tradition with which I am primarily concerned here[139] has in fact produced new perspectives or brought them to light again. I would like to draw particular attention at this point to two women, exegetes, because they both begin from a clearly formulated concern to allow the vanished women to speak again, and in so doing make further use of theoretical methodology: Bernadette Brooten and Elisabeth Schüssler-Fiorenza.[140] To this end I shall quote an example from the work of Bernadette Brooten which in the meantime has already become quite well-known. In Romans 16, in the list of greetings, Paul gives two names, Andronicus and Junia. He describes them as 'kinsfolk' (so they, too, were Jews) and fellow prisoners, of note among the apostles (v.7). Bernadette Brooten has worked out the tradition history of this text and come to the following result: Junia does not now appear as a feminine name either in the critical edition of the Greek Nestle text nor in the translations. Instead, Junias is written, which would have to be a Graecized and abbreviated form of a male Latin name Iunianus. But there is no evidence of such a name, even in non-biblical texts, while there is for the female name Junia. Junia is attested by the Chester Beatty Papyrus of the third century, in other words the earliest manuscript that we possess for the New Testament letters, but from the thirteenth century it is 'refantasized' into the male name Junias. The later history is also interesting. The much calumniated church fathers preserve the feminine form. Brooten cites John Chrysostom, to whom Mary Daly gives a place in her 'chamber of horrors' of misogynist church fathers, but who still has more interest in dealing honestly with the tradition than in deleting women: 'There is something great about being an apostle. But to be pre-eminent among the apostles – think what marvellous praise that is. They were pre-eminent by virtue of their work and their honest tasks. How great the wisdom of this woman must have been for her to have been found worthy of the title apostle.'[141] The last link in the chain of this historical development is that the latest edition of the Greek text of Nestle has deleted the feminine variant of the name from the critical apparatus altogether. Anyone who works only with this text will no longer find even the problem.[142]

The interest in making women disappear from the tradition can be unthinking in that the men who are active in writing history are not interested in the women in this history. Here the specific sexual determination of people would be the principle of selection for their activity quite prior to any possible evil intent. Another example should show that intentions can also play a part here. This time, however, it was not a woman but a man who investigated the history of the tradition of a text, namely Adolf von Harnack. By citing him I would also like to show that I am primarly concerned with the interest of a person and not with his or her sex.

In 1900 Harnack published an article[143] which was concerned with another 'prominent' woman in the New Testament, Prisca or, as she is also called, Priscilla. Prisca and her husband Aquila are mentioned in the letters of the apostle Paul and in Acts. On the basis of the scant mentions in the text[144] we can reconstruct the following picture. The couple Prisca and Aquila – most of the time she is mentioned before her husband, which indicates her significance, come from Pontus on the Black Sea. Both are of Jewish descent and live in Rome. Aquila is a craftsman by profession, as is Paul. As a result of an edict of the Emperor Claudius of AD 49 Jews and, because the emperor could not understand the difference, also Jewish Christians were expelled from the city. At the time of the edict Prisca and Aquila were probably already Christians. The couple fled to Corinth and settled there. Paul got to know them in Corinth and worked for a while in Aquila's workshop. The couple travelled on with Paul to Asia Minor in the service of the mission, settled in Ephesus, and there founded a house community, but Paul journeyed further. The Jewish-Christian Apollos from Alexandria was introduced more fully into the truth of the Christian faith by the couple, which means that he was also taught by Prisca (Acts 18.2,18,26; cf. I Cor.16.19; Rom.16.3). I have quoted only Acts because the further history of this text is particularly interesting. The Syro-Latin recension and Codex D (the so-called 'Western text') change the Alexandrian version (Codex A) in 18.2 from 'he (Paul) found there (Corinth) Aquila *and* his wife Priscilla' to 'Aquila *with* his wife Priscilla'. That in itself does not seem to be a very serious change. But it goes on: 'He went to *them*' (Codex A) which is changed by the Western text into 'he went to *him*' (i.e. Aquila alone). According to Codex A it is said that 'Prisca and Aquila heard Apollos', but the Western text changes the order of the names to 'Aquila and Prisca'. In three verses the Western text inserts a sole mention of Aquila, shifting the emphasis in favour of the husband. But in so doing it destroys the significance of the statements of the text in their context. Verse 3 inserts 'but Paul knew Aquila', which in view of what has gone before is an unnecessary observation; in v.7 Codex D adds 'and he went away from Aquila'. But Paul does not go away from Aquila; he does not change his abode, but because of hostility from the synagogue he goes into the house of Titius Justus which was next to the synagogue. In v.21 the Western text repeats v.9 with a mention of Aquila: 'he left Aquila behind in Ephesus' is inserted. Verse 27 says that Apollos, having been taught by Prisca and Aquila, wants to travel from Ephesus to Achaea: 'The brethren' (Prisca and Aquila are not mentioned here by name but included among the fellow-Christians in their house community by means of the word 'brethren') write a letter of commendation so that Apollos will be well received in Achaea. Even that is evidently too much stress on the couple and their house community for the Western text. So it enlarges on the 'brethren': it is Corinthians in Ephesus (who happen to be staying there but are not members of the house community) who determine that Apollos should travel on. According to Codex D it is not Prisca and Aquila who write the letter, but 'the Ephesians'. Finally, Tertullian (c.AD 200) mentions Aquila but not Prisca among those who served Paul well, in a letter which is concerned with the question whether one may flee in situations of persecution.[145]

Such laborious work on details brings out tendencies which indicate an interest in making women vanish. That this sort of thing happens even now will emerge from the third and last instance, which calls for not so much labour, but for heightened awareness. I am referring to two sources: in 1983 there appeared in the famous series Quaestiones Disputatae, published by Herder Verlag, a book entitled 'Women in Earliest Christianity';[146] three years earlier a collection entitled 'Traditions of Liberation. Women in the Bible' had been co-published by Kaiser and Burckhardthaus-Laetare.[147] The first of these books, also a collection, and dedicated to Rudolf Schnackenburg on his sixty-fifth birthday by a group of Catholic pupils who are exegetes, claims in the Foreword to have the aim of clarifying the 'increasing obscuring of the equality of men and women in Christ',[148] which had already taken place in the course of history that the New Testament canon represents. Two women authors were represented in it: one, Magdalena Bussmann, commented on these concerns as a sign that men 'help to the best of their ability'.[149]

Anyone who shares this interest breathes again and is warmly delighted at the concern for reconciliation, cooperation against the competition which is often experienced.

Now anyone who does not also pick up the second book can continue to be delighted and hopeful. Elisabeth Schüssler-Fiorenza is in fact also a pupil of Schnackenburg's and to begin with was a contributor to the Herder Festschrift. However, her contribution did not appear in this book but in the second one,[150] as the editors of the Herder volume rejected it, although they had originally promised to publish it. The reason was that what Elisabeth Schüssler-Fiorenza said 'had too explosive associations with current issues'.[151] Since when, the reader may ask, may academic study not be topical? Since when has scholarship been afraid of a possible controversy (and when I compared the articles, I did not find the latter one anything like as controversial as I had expected)? The reasons for such a procedure must therefore lie elsewhere. They are not manifest, but can be read out of the interest that could already be seen in the biblical texts, namely in keeping women quiet.

Keeping unpopular people quiet is a well known and standard practice[152] in totalitarian states and thus a form of violence. The interest of women in not being kept quiet does not have to be legitimated first, since interest does not need any kind of legitimation. It is simply there. In the case of women it came immediately into view. We do not need the church fathers to get the creeps. Quite apart from that, interest is always determined by present experience. The suppression of a woman from an academic sphere of activity is a characteristic example of a way of proceeding which is matched by many more serious violations: the oppressive extent of violence against women, open and hidden, practised by strangers or by husbands, fathers and other close relations, against adult women, and also against children, is only now slowly coming to public view.[153] Social justice towards women is nowhere achieved: in many spheres of work the relationship between work and pay is not the decisive factor, but the relationship between sex and pay. Women do most of the 'shadow work',[154] to the detriment of their health. Women are usually punished more harshly than men for criminal offences.[155]

In view of these experiences, which are noted far too little, if at all, by the churches (and they do not relate only to the so-called 'lower classes'), any sermon, any quotation about the servitude of women, their alleged ethical inadequacy, their role as a stimulation to male desire must appear to be sheer cynicism, namely in the way in which it so often speaks sweepingly of 'women'. The experience of being regarded as inferior, if not in fact being treated as such, is brought out by the growing flood of women's literature. Athough formally rights are equal, in the professions the emotional and therefore also the actual barriers are still great enough. And finally, the struggle of women for ordination in Protestant churches has only achieved its aim in very recent years, while in their Roman Catholic sister church resignation and perplexity are widespread. Women can indeed acquire the same qualifications as theologians, and no one seriously wants to meddle with the working of the Holy Spirit and deny the possibility that the Spirit also calls women; nevertheless, because Jesus was a man only men can be active as priests.[156]

Towards the transcending of feminist theology

There is no doubt that eroticism and responsibility, social justice and indeed the comprehensive claims of care and bringing up children are human problems. But instead of getting helpful efforts towards a solution, women experience violence and rejection. These are experiences which must be taken seriously, even if they do not affect every woman, or each one to the same extent. This is the source of all feminist interest and what is a primarily irrational reaction.

The fight by feminists against method, science, reason, against everything that has to do with the head, represents a resistance which on closer inspection has always been more or less markedly present in history. This problem, too, can be elucidated in terms of the sociology of knowledge. Human beings are simultaneously experiencing and reflective subjects,[157] and in its specific form their history is the consequence of 'the hidden connection between thought and reality – the essential identity of subject and object'.[158] Karl Mannheim calls the opposed pair, which do not work out without each other and therefore cannot be separated, life and spirit.[159] 'Spirit and life point to two basically different ways of experiencing the world...'[160] Any rational illumination of historical reality goes hand in hand 'with the potentialities of the whole person and his or her action which reach forward, at first in a tentative way, irrational, spiritual and psychological.'[161] Seeing this connection is an important consequence of theoretical reflection, for anyone who appeals only to one side does violence to the other, the rationalist to the irrational element in human consciousness and the irrationalist to the rational element. In both instances a totality is torn apart,[162] and 'rationalism and irrationalism, construction and intuition, concept and view... are played off against each other as though they were slogans.'[163] The one side thus has no advantage over the other.

The use of reason is always the second step after the first stage of irrational outburst, which expresses vital interest. The origin of historical-critical exegesis might be mentioned as an example. Every theologian now learns in his or her study the methods of historical-critical work which were developed over decades and which were also, indeed particularly, worked out in connection with biblical texts. This business of exegesis is done in a sober and rational way, and not only the outsider finds it dispassionate and laborious. However, the origin of these methods, which are now acknowledged and established, derives from a passionate interest: the battle against the captivity of thought to church dogma. 'The quest of the historical Jesus,' a first and decisive undertaking of historical-critical thought, 'did not take its rise from a purely historical interest; it turned to the Jesus of history as an ally in the struggle against the tyranny of dogma.'[164] All those who went in search of the historical Jesus lavished on him all the hatred and all the love of which they were capable. This was not hatred of the person of Jesus, Albert Schweitzer went on to write, but hatred of the supernatural nimbus with which he had been surrounded, so that it was impossible to enter into a relationship with the man from Galilee. The scandal of the irrational outburst furthered history and science.[165] Thus irrationality and rationality are connected. And Albert Schweitzer developed this notion again very vividly: 'It is strange to notice how often in the history of our subject a few imperfectly equipped free-lances have attacked and attempted to carry the decisive positions before the ordered ranks of professional theology have pushed their advance too these decisive points.'[166] The structural parallel between passionate interest and hatred of feminist irrationality is manifest. Also behind this hatred an almost, or completely, concealed hope of breaking through the 'dogmatic' nimbus of the man in order to be able to share life with him may be at work.

The second step after the first stage of irrational outburst is the use of reason, reflection, since there is an inner relationship between willing and knowing, subjective interest and the question how that which was presented to us by history is possible; both are parts of the same totality.[167] I have already discussed this side of the problem.[168] In addition there is something further, which indicates why reason, objectification and theorization are important. Without reflective and theorizing detachment we are delivered over to the perplexities of reality. True, we are always directly in a historical situation, but we have to define it. 'It is, if not our own creation, nevertheless something that we have to define. And such a "definition" of the environment represents the way in which we "come to terms" with it.'[169] The fact that science, the sciences, with their manifold methods, have come into existence is not to be seen either as chance or as a bad patriarchalist joke. The claim to reflection, the concern for objectification, the ability to become detached from the forms of immediacy in experience and action are what make purposeful consideration and responsible action possible. The objectification of interest allows us to see more clearly the historical complex of effects in which we stand; research into the historical complex of effects in turn enables us to become more clearly aware of our own interest. All this illuminates the complex of communication in which we do stand, and to which we fall victim the more easily if we do not see through it and consequently lose our sense of direction. There was recentlly in Vienna an example of this kind of losing a sense of direction: Edit Schlaffer, well known for her radical feminist publications, got married, and her ecumenical wedding caused something of a stir. In the view of Edit Schlaffer femininity as a sacrificial attitude had been fixed not least by a long Christian tradition for which Paul in particular was responsible as a propagandist.[170] So she inexorably challenged men with the contradiction between theory and practice.[171] That is just one of the many attacks on Christianity when it is identified with patriarchalism. So why a church wedding? A disappointed feminist reacted, among other things, with the ironic suggestion that it would have been to risky for Edit Schlaffer 'to live all alone with a man if God was not there'.[172]

A third reason for the significance of critical reflection is shown by the further development of historical-critical research, which has already been mentioned. One result of the initial irrational impetus was 'eisegesis', reading one's own interest on to the person of Jesus. Every era of theology, every individual rediscovered their ideas in Jesus and so created him in accordance with their own personality.[173] Once the passion had sobered down it proved possible to grasp the figure of Jesus from his own history. In this sense there is a possibility of 'also finding a measurement and representation of past eras on the basis of their own criteria and values'.[174] However, this would not have any connection with a particular present unless at the same time it also disclosed the alien factor which governs history. Only the critical analysis of historical texts which deliberately leaves aside its own interest can bring this out or rediscover it as the result of a confrontation. 'If the text is to have anything to say again, there is a need for a rediscovery of the text by reading it against the grain.'[175] Thus history can again arouse new interest through the alien nature of its testimony. Moreover this method of distancing is capable of being criticized in the face of other interests and one's own in the name of fairness, so that the complex of communication does not fall apart for both sides to exploit.

The next chapters are meant to be understood in the light of this dialectic of interest and readiness to put oneself in question by results obtained from looking through the tradition. I am deliberately taking up themes which have already been worked on and brought to public attention in the context of feminist theology. In the conviction that the phase of irrational outcry is and must be detached from the next stage of sober critical examination if the outcry is really to make its effect on history, my interest is also directed towards the examination of previous arguments from feminist theological positions.[176]

The goal which lies before us is the transcending of feminism and feminist theology. Feminist theology is as nonsensical a concept as a theology of liberation, of hope, of questioning and so on. Would theology be conceivable at all without questioning and searching, without hope, without the freedom of the children of God, without women and without a humane relationship between the sexes? The fact that such demarcations nevertheless arise is a sign that elements without which theology would not be theology have lost their significance and must be regained. As long as women have to make themselves and their overgrown history the object of investigations, as long as they call for the institutionalization of feminist research, demand teaching posts for it and other things, all is not in order. Anything that was quite naturally worked on by women and men together with equal concern would not have to be stressed by a special term like feminist theology. That in accordance with Gal.3.28 there is neither man nor women should also apply to the pursuit of theology. So a feminist theology first of all remains a sign that a common way together has still to be found.

From this there emerges the goal of the transcending of feminist theology, and that means that one day it will become superfluous. Historical-critical research, which has been so regularly referred to here, also found its meaningful and necessary place in theology. As a result, historical method gained in accuracy and effectiveness; as a result, theology was reorganized and changed. In this the original interest in being freed from the monopoly of dogma was not lost, but remains a permanent challenge to produce a connection between two conflicting forces. Should that not also be possible for feminist theology?

CHAPTER THREE

In the Steps of Jesus

The New Testament is regarded as the criterion for what is Christian. For a feminist theology which does not want to give up its relationship to this tradition that means a challenge to assess or correct the present significance of women in and for theology and the church by means of this criterion.

Now the canon is not a book of doctrinal statements but depicts the history of human beings and their relationship to God. The New Testament presents the history of the origin of Christian faith and is regarded as the beginning, authorized by the church, through which it has committed itself. All movements which have been critical of the church, however successful, heretical or capable of adaptation, refer to the Bible and reinterpret it; they set their new certainty that they have understood the text rightly over against the traditional and familiar understanding. To this degree the Bible has always also proved to be a dangerous book. The impulses towards asking of the biblical texts what things were like at the beginning come from the experience at a given time that the church is alienated from its beginning; in other words they arise from a contradiction which gives rise to an interest in investigation.

So it is not surprising that Christian women should investigate the beginnings of the church in the light of their negative experiences and want to know whether what they experience in the churches today, or what is mediated through a Christian understanding, coincides with things as they were at the beginning. And as Jesus of Nazareth, the Christ, stands at the centre of the New Testament, it is not surprising that they should want to know who Jesus was, and how, as a man, he dealt with women. So the theme of 'Jesus and the women' recurs very frequently in feminist theology.

Jesus – the man of feminist dreams

Jesus the 'integrated' man – this was the concept which Hanna Wolff attempted to use in 1975 to in order to understand the person of Jesus by interpreting him in terms of Jung's archetypes.[177] 'Integrated' means that Jesus was reconciled with his anima, the feminine archetype in his unconscious. 'The feminine is no longer just the enemy to be fought against, nor is it any longer a symbol of infantility. It has become, rather, the ontic basic possibility of existence in which male existence participates in exactly the same way as feminine existence.'[178] What is the basis for Hanna Wolff's judgment? 'Now, Jesus's closer and wider environment had an androcentric or patriarchal orientation. It was dominated by the animus. Jesus was not. Jesus is the great exception... In his encounter with women Jesus shows spontaneous understanding, he is without resentment: rather, he is a partner in their concerns... He was persecuted not least for this attitude; it became his destiny.'[179]

Hanna Wolff's interpretation has constantly been seized on by feminists with delight, as it combines criticism of patriarchalism with reconciliation between the sexes. Nevertheless, critical questions emerge:

1. Hanna Wolff's stress on the uniqueness of Jesus in dealing with women is meant to be a historical judgment. As such, however, it comes up against considerable difficulties, since there are good reasons for regarding as a failure the attempt of the quest of the historical Jesus to understand Jesus as the person that he really was. First, the sources are too sparse and too strongly stamped by the interest of faith, and secondly, the interest of the recipient easily falsifies the historical evidence; like all those in quest of the historical Jesus, Hanna Wolff's interest causes her to read things into the evidence. This judgment is confirmed by the way in which in so many other respects Jesus is already said to have been unique in the historical sense. He had already been regarded as just about everything: the unique and immaculate embodiment of true virtue, a member of a secret society, a miracle

worker endowed with special powers, a revolutionary, a failed
Reformer, and now the 'integrated' man and friend of women.
Any view can be attested by texts – and that has indeed been
attempted. This state of affairs makes one sceptical. Hanna Wolff
could have found better arguments had she attempted to justify
her judgment in dogmatic terms: the uniqueness of Jesus as the
Son of God endorses the claim of faith that there is no respect of
persons with God, neither man nor woman...(Gal.3.28). The
degree to which Hanna Wolff reads her own interest into texts
can also be seen from her terminology, as when she talks of
'objective partnership'. As we shall see, there can be other reasons
for the way in which Jesus dealt with women.

2. Partnership is not a term from the world in which Jesus lived,
any more than are terms like archetype, animus and anima.
However, there is a close connection between language, the
formation of concepts and therefore states of consciousness and
the realities of life. Knowledge determines action, perception, the
world of conception. All human activity goes through the filter of
consciousness as the place where theories are formed – in the
broadest sense. A psychoanalyst sees reality with different eyes
from those of an itinerant preacher in the first century. So since
the theory of the unconscious and of archetypes belongs to the
twentieth century, and not to the first, it is questionable whether
someone who lived so long ago can be understood as he was at
that time. The psychoanalytical interpretation does not take into
account the specific historical situation. Jesus and the people of
his time stand in a history which differs in many respects from
the reality of our experience. Hanna Wolff is certainly aware of
this, but she does not draw any consequences from it.[180]

3. In terms of content, the theory of the anima in the male
unconscious and the animus in the female unconscious, the
premise from which Jung begins, in other words for which he
gives no further justification, can be defined more closely: 'The
male mode of coping with existence is... coming to himself in a
way which extends from him and beyond him in that he in fact
assumes responsibility or faces it. The feminine mode of existence
is by contrast a being-present in being itself, in we-ness, in being
together in mutual giving and receiving.'[181] In this sentence Hanna
Wolff is not quoting Jung but the anthropologist F.J.J.Buytendijk,

and that is illuminating: Buytendijk does not in fact speak of extra-historical archetypes but of existence, and of male and female modes as anthropological factors. Hanna Wolff herself makes the connection with Jung, from which it can be concluded that the definition of the content of the archetypes gained from the nature of the man or of the woman and thus historical experience become a postulate independent of history; in this way the widespread prejudgment of an unchangeable male and female 'essence' without historical and individual differentiation, is elevated into something 'valid in and for itself'. Jung's archetypes correspond to the hypothesis of the eternal feminine and the eternal masculine. So either the eternal idea does violence to reality, or reality, without justification, presumes to be the unshakable criterion through all ages and cultures. Anyone who believes that will also depict reality accordingly, but anyone who wants to learn something beyond himself or herself must renounce such methods. Injustice should not be done to Jung and his followers, and therefore it should be pointed out that Jung makes a distinction between the interpretation of the archetype and its representation in reality: no human being corresponds on the basis of his or her natural sex to just one mode, the male or the female. Anyone, whether man or woman, participates in both archetypes, and if social usage seeks to fix him or her to one corresponding to natural sex, the result is the disintegration of the individual. On the contrary, in contrast to social usage, the goal is integration, the affirmation of the archetype which does not correspond to the natural sex and which is anchored in the unconsciousness of any individual. But that does not do away with the three points of criticism already mentioned, in which the archetype theory, as also in the version of it by Erich Neumann, must cope with increasing feminist counter-arguments.[182]

Elisabeth Moltmann-Wendel wants to see Jesus as the 'tender' man.[183] She asks about 'private relationships', asks herself whether 'sexual intercourse' did not take place between Jesus and Mary Magdalene, and dreams with Ernst Eggimann of the overcoming of morality by Jesus and his relationship with Mary Magdalene. She praises the Gospel of Mark because, for example, it expresses 'physical nearness' in the accounts of healings and has handed on to us the tender Jesus.[184] Again the problem is whether it is possible to rediscover the historical man Jesus. The touching of people by charismatic healers is not something specific to Jesus. The laying on of hands was one of the ritual practices customary at that time. The fact that Mary Magdalene was one of the closest followers of Jesus is far from implying 'sexual intercourse', any more than the fact that the beloved disciple reclined on Jesus' breast (John 13.23) can allow us to conclude that Jesus had homosexual relationships. All the wishes which have already been projected on to Jesus in sexual matters produce an extremely confusing picture. The conceptuality of Elisabeth Moltmann – private relationships, sexual intercourse, new morality, physical proximity, tenderness – also shows the present interest which begins from the experience of the final differentiation of sensibilities – human beings in our day find it hard to imagine love without sexuality. Associations with the biblical texts remain associative fantasy. Fantasy is fine, but one should not think that it is a way towards discovering a history which has long lain in the past. Such procedures misuse the canon in a totally unthought-out way to legitimate one's own interests.

The significance of the context

Anyone who investigates women in the New Testament gets a dusty answer: some names are mentioned, and in a few cases a little more than that. The authors of the biblical writings have no interest in biographies; as men, moreover, they are more interested in their own history.[185] Therefore I shall not make any attempt at biographical reconstruction. In what follows I want to depict the context which was significant for Jesus and his men and women followers, and in the light of that to understand them, along with all that is alien to us. In so doing I shall refer not only to biblical but also to extra-biblical sources.[186] In terms of method I shall base myself on a sociological analysis, albeit in terms of the position in the sociology of knowledge which I have already described, as a reciprocal relationship between theory and praxis, consciousness and reality, interest and the resistance of 'what is fact'[187], already in history itself.

Jesus and his followers were one of many renewal movements within Judaism which were condemned by outsiders as heretical.

Where were the grounds for such renewal movements and what made the Jesus group special? The area of Palestine at the beginning of our era was a political and social crisis area of the first order. That was connected with the expansion of the Roman empire or the conditions it produced and with the history of the Jewish people, which from the very beginning had ascribed itself a privileged role among the peoples but which for centuries had already had to suffer under more or less tolerant foreign rule. Therefore in assessing the Jesus tradition it is important to use as a criterion not only the Old Testament but also the inter-testamental period, which reveals particular developments over against the tradition documented in the Old Testament. Thus for example while the Israelite monarchy had long been replaced by a priestly theocracy, large circles of Judaism showed themselves open to Hellenism, while others fought against this development; there were marked tensions between Jerusalem and Galilee and between city and country.

I shall now demonstrate this crisis situation more closely in terms of the burden of taxation, though I would not want to make taxes exclusively responsible for everything. Nevertheless it is always economic crises which increase tensions of many kinds, since here the most vital interests are infringed. At the time of Jesus the Jews lived in a territory occupied by the Romans and had to pay a mass of taxes to the occupying authorities: every year about a quarter of the crop, land and poll tax (*tributum solis et capitis*) and in addition offerings in kind (*annona*) and unpaid services for the occupation forces, customs duty, and tolls for using the roads. Agriculture and therefore land was the economic basis of Palestine, so it was here that most was to be had. That applied not only to taxes but also to the confiscation of property, a practice carried out by both the Roman and the Jewish authorities, dependent on Roman favour, and necessary for gifts, bribes or for the settlement of retired Roman legionaries. The increasing impoverishment of the small farmers and the accumulation of possessions in the hands of the great landowners meant that the poor got increasingly poor and the rich got increasingly rich. There is some such experience behind the statement in the Gospel of Luke (19.26): 'To him who has it shall be given and from him who has not shall be taken away even what he has.'

Political tensions could lead to remissions in taxes but also to increases in taxes, and this was rightly understood by the Jews as punishment for their intractability. The pressure of taxation also makes it clear why publicans were so hated. As tax farmers they worked for the Romans; they not only levied the taxes for them, but in so doing also betrayed the Jewish resistance against Rome. The burden of taxation and debt was further 'enhanced' by bad harvests, famine and epidemics, especially in the 20s and 60s of the first century. so it is not surprising that criticism of the rich runs through the Jesus tradition like a scarlet thread, and that the remission of debts is given a positive interpretation, indeed becomes a parable for the grace of God (e.g. Luke 16.1ff.).

The impoverished farmers and small tenants often faced the choice of either going into slavery for debt or running away by turning their backs on any form of social order, in the style of desperadoes. There is evidence for robbers and beggars in this period, and for long afterwards in the Roman Empire; here, like Robin Hood, they felt that right was on their side in that they were taking back from the rich what they themselves had lost through injustice. In Italy the robber captain Bulla (end of the second century) achieved fame, as reported by the historian Dio Cassius, by retorting to a centurion: 'Tell your masters that they must give their servants enough to live on so that they do not have to become robbers.' When Bulla had finally been captured the leader of the troop asked him why he was a robber. 'Why are you leader of a troop?' was the robber's succinct answer; for they were both robbers, the desperadoes and the officials of an exploitative state.[188]

The social phenomenon of 'rootlessness'[189] was also associated with religious motives – necessarily so because of the connection between reality and consciousness. For example, the radical Zealots[190] fought for liberation from foreign rule and refused to pay taxes because of their belief in a Messiah whom God would send to redeem Israel from the hands of the Romans. They organized resistance in the hills and in so doing attempted to impose their political messianism with force. Finally they became the tragic victims of Roman superiority, and Jerusalem fell with them (AD 70). Before the capture of the last Zealot outpost, the fortress of Masada, their leader Eleazar, with his fellow-fighters

and their wives and children, committed suicide so as not to fall
into the cruel hands of the Romans. Eleazar begins his speech by
describing how the Zealots understood themselves. 'My brave
comrades, since long ago we resolved never to be subject to the
Romans, nor to any other than God himself, who is the true and
just Lord of mankind.'[191]

The question of taxation for the Emperor (Mark 12.13-17 par.)
links this theme to the Jesus tradition. It was above all followers
of Herod, including Pharisees, not part of the opposition over the
question of taxation, who wanted to lure Jesus on to thin ice. 'Is
it lawful to pay tax to Caesar or not?' ran the trick question. If
Jesus said 'Yes, it is lawful', he showed himself to be pro-Roman
and against the Jewish tradition and the suffering people. If he
said, 'No, it is unlawful', he declared himself to be a Zealot and
resistance fighter and gave himself into the hands of the Roman
aggressors or their Jewish instruments. No matter which way he
answered, he fell into the trap. His answer that the Emperor and
God should each be given their own does not just mean that he
was able to avoid the trap – which would simply make him
cunning; this answer also accords with his conviction and his way
of life. He was not interested in taxes, since he and his followers
were not faced with the question whether or not to pay them.
They had nothing. They had long since avoided such problems
by another life-style.

Jesus' attitude indicates that anyone who has anything must
pay taxes to Caesar, but anyone who wants to give to God what
is God's, namely his whole life, should renounce possessions and
– one could add along the lines of Mark 10.17-31 – 'follow
me'. By asking for a coin before he adopts his position Jesus
demonstrates publicly that he has no possessions. The church
father Ambrose, Bishop of Milan in the fourth century, comments
on this pericope in the Gospel of Luke: 'He did not give of what
he had, but he gave back to the world what belonged to it. If you
do not want to be obligated to the emperor, do not wish for what
belongs to the world. But if you have riches you are indebted to
the emperor. If you do not want to be indebted to the earthly king,
leave all you have and follow Christ.'[192]

Jesus and his followers lived as itinerant preachers. They went
around through the cities and villages, and preached conversion

of heart and the imminence of the kingdom of God which opposes its criteria to all earthly riches. This form of life and its religious motivation are most aptly expressed in the mission charge to the disciples (Matt.10.7-16), which has continually caused men and women to change their way of life, not least Francis of Assisi. 'Preach as you go, saying "The kingdom of God is at hand." Heal the sick, raise the dead, cleanse the lepers, drive out demons. You received (charismata, gifts) freely, give freely. Take neither gold, silver nor copper in your belts; no bag (for provisions or begging) on your journey, no second garment (i.e. a change of clothing = luxury), nor shoes nor a staff (as a weapon = sign of a peaceful intent); for the labourer is worthy of his hire. And when you go into a town or a village find out who is worthy in it; remain there until you leave again. When you enter a house greet it lovingly, and if the house is worthy of you, your wish for its peace will come true. But if it is not worthy, your wish for peace will come back to you. And if any one will not receive either you or your words, leave that house or that city and shake the dust from off your feet.'[193]

Many other texts also attest that Jesus and his followers led such an itinerant life without possessions: anyone who hears the call to discipleship leaves behind house (home), brothers, sisters, mother, father, children and fields (land) (Mark 10.29); the foxes have holes and the birds nests, but the Son of Man (Jesus) has nowhere to lay his head (Matt.8.20); the life of the itinerant preacher is compared with the lilies of the field who do not reap and sow and yet are fed by their heavenly Father (Matt.6.25ff.). The rich man in Mark 10.17ff. could not be separated from his possessions. So it is easier for a camel to go through the eye of a needle than for a rich man to enter the kingdom of God.

The 'service' of the women

What did the group around Jesus live on if they themselves had nothing? Three possible sources can be reconstructed. First, from the food offered them by the friendly houses that they entered. This would be more likely to be gifts in kind than money. Secondly, they had hospitality in the homes of their families, as long as there was some contact with them, as e.g. in the case of Peter's family

(Mark 1.30-31) or in the group of close families, 'sympathizers',[194] as e.g. in the house of Mary and Martha (Luke 10.38ff.). Thirdly, it may be that rich people who decided to become disciples possibly brought their possessions into the group, though whether totally or in part must remain an open question (Luke 8.3). Such a practice is also reflected in the Acts of the Apostles, though the formation of local Christian communities was already well under way in this period: everyone held everything in common (Acts 4.32). It is said of Ananias and Sapphira that they sold their possessions to lay the proceeds 'at the feet' of the apostles in the earliest community, so that they could be distributed within the community. But they then yielded to the temptation to keep some for themselves, so they dropped down dead as a punishment (Acts 5). The death penalty for keeping one's own possessions – that shows how significant being without possessions remained in the local communities.[195]

We now come up against the women around Jesus. In the Gospel of Luke (8.1-3) women are mentioned in addition to the Twelve, three of them by name: Mary Magdalene, Johanna and Susanna. They had been healed by Jesus and 'cared for them with the possessions that they had' (v.3), a reference to property and income. One of the women, Johanna, was the wife of an official at the court of King Herod and was therefore certainly not poor. Had she left her husband and brought her share of the property with her? At all events she is not said to be a widow, though a number of theologians would like to read that into her position to maintain family morality.[196] But any kind of suppositions about Johanna's marriage remain speculation. Despite the views of Luise Schottroff,[197] it is quite in keeping with the life-style of Jesus and his followers that these women, not just Joanna, should have supported the Jesus group by giving them provisions, if we begin from the fact that it did not mean riches and possessions for the group but the possibility of living for a while on what had been given them until it was used up.

In view of the life-style of the group another interpretation is absurd: Josef Blank thinks '...that women... took on the task of looking after Jesus and his disciples day by day'.[198] What do we understand by 'looking after' here? Cooking? Where? Washing, when there was no change of clothing? Bodily care with a view to the imminence of the kingdom of God? Moreover, such an interpretation fails to see that the text explicitly says that the women looked after the needs of the group with their possessions. But Josef Blank would prefer to keep to the idea of 'daily care', and thus is a good example of the way in which personal interest can turn exegesis into eisegesis.

In commentaries on this text one continually finds the observation that the women who followed Jesus did not take part in preaching and in this respect differed from the male followers.[199] On the other hand v.1 says explicitly that Jesus proclaimed the good news of the kingdom of God 'and the twelve with him and some women who...' The connection between discipleship and proclamation is already brought out equally for men and women in this first sentence. That is endorsed by comparison with the scene of the women under the cross (Mark 15.20-21), '...who when he (Jesus) was in Galilee followed him and served him.' 'Following' in all the texts is a technical term for complete participation in the conviction and activity of the travelling preachers. That the women in Luke 8 were 'sympathetic families' has not the slightest support in the text.[200]

In Luke 8 the word 'serve' is identified with possessions and therefore with a kind of material support for daily needs. But even where this connection does not appear, as for example in the passion narrative, it would be a mistake in the light of the overall context to see the serving as specifically feminine household activity. For the kingdom of God is characterized by its diametrical opposition to all the kingdoms of this earth. It is a reality over against what is customary and usual. Whereas in the kingdoms of the world princes and kings rule and exercise authority, there is no rule in the kingdom of God, but service: 'But it shall not be so among you; but whoever would be great among you must be your servant, and whoever would be first among you must be slave of all; for the Son of man also came not to be served but to serve...'(Mark 10.43-45).

On the basis of their conviction of the coming kingdom of God Jesus and his followers practised a life-style in accord with this conviction, which freed people from the manifold contradictions of existence. The group is 'inclusive',[201] as it does not have criteria which exclude people but criteria the conditions of which must be fulfilled when people join it. So it is not a question of: no rich, no Zealot, no publican, no harlot, no Pharisee, no woman... but: any rich person, any Zealot, any publican, any whore, any Pharisee, any woman, as long as they share this conviction and the life-style of the group. It is not the past that counts but now, orientated on a new future.

The beginning of the history of Christianity thus offers a different picture of the estimation of women from that which later tradition has continually shown down to the present day. Nevertheless, its alien features are clear: we do not travel around, we are not homeless, without possessions or even inspired by the deep conviction that the kingdom of God and thus the revaluation of all traditional values will come. Our century is stamped by a different history from that in which it all began. A purely biographical approach to the women in the New Testament cannot grasp the complex reality of their lives, and brings it nearer to us than would be honest.

A striking feature of the Jesus tradition is its marked hostility to the family. Before Jesus gathered his own group around him he had been a member of the group around John the Baptist, had had himself baptized by John and later separated from him. Hostility to the family is already a theme in the Baptist tradition: 'Do not presume to say to yourselves, "We have Abraham as our father"; for I tell you, God is able from these stones to raise up children to Abraham' (Matt.3.9). This passage from the preaching of John the Baptist says that anyone who refers to genealogy and blood relationship in matters of faith and relations to God does not know what these are about. The fact that Abraham, too, was elect of God is far from meaning that those who descend from him physically are also elect. The relationship to God cannot be inherited. Everyone must be challenged by the call to repentance and make a decision.

Jesus continually stresses that the 'true' family is represented by those bound together in common conviction and not physical relationship. In Mark 3.31-35 we are told how the mother and brothers of Jesus, who is surrounded and protected by a crowd of people, call for him. The people draw the attention of Jesus to the approach of his kinsfolk, but he turns them back and replies that his mother, brothers and sisters are all those who throng round him and listen to him. Being bound in faith is regarded as the decisive factor in the Jesus group: blood ties are unimportant.

His own family evidently did not join Jesus. According to Mark 3.20-27 the relatives hear of the great press of people around Jesus and make an attempt to lay hands on him. They think that he is beside himself, out of his senses, not normal. Here the attitude of Jesus' kinsfolk, which probably must also be taken to include his mother, are at one with the attitude of his enemies who accuse him of being possessed by Beelzebul.

Mark 6.1-6 points in the same direction. Jesus teaches in the synagogue of his home town of Nazareth. Again the question of his legitimation arises. Whence does he get what he says? We know his family, his mother – the father is not mentioned and we do not know whether he had already died by then – his brothers and his sisters who behave quite 'normally'.[202] The question 'Whence does he get it?' can be answered in three ways: from human beings, i.e. from some teaching authority, from God or from Beelzebul. Jesus himself appeals solely and directly to God. Precisely because people in Nazareth know his origins, they do not believe his call. Since Jesus meets with no trust, no faith, he has no power; for example he cannot heal. Again blood affinity stands over against faith.

Opinions divide sharply over whom Jesus represents, for and against. Luke 12.49-53 gives a vivid picture of this: Jesus has not come to bring peace on earth but division. In one house father and son, mother and daughter, mother-in-law and daughter-in-law, will be in conflict. Where common conviction and life-style do not hold them together, the ties of kindred too, indeed particularly, will fail. The saying in Luke 14.26 is even harsher by virtue of its call to action: 'If someone comes to me and does not hate father and mother, wife and children, brothers and sisters... he cannot be my disciple.'[203] The calls to discipleship imply turning away from what so far has been one's family so that one cannot be delayed by such an incidental matter as burying one's father (Matt.8.22).

Again inclusiveness and not exclusiveness is the criterion: following Jesus separates one from kinsfolk who do not under-stand what it is all about. But to be related to someone does not exclude following Jesus, in so far as these kinsfolk are bound together in common conviction over and above family ties. So among the disciples of Jesus there are the two sons of Zebedee, i.e. brothers. However, the basic presupposition remains the common conviction which creates new forms of society. All others come under what Jesus says to a 'woman from the people' who praises the body and breasts of his mother: 'Rather, blessed are those who hear the word of God and do it' (Luke 11.27-28).

Such textual material and a comparison with the life-style of itinerant Cynic philosophers who also went through the land and lived unmarried have been and are[204] taken as a basis for supposing that the Jesus group did not marry. This thesis is confirmed above all by Luke, who, in contrast to Mark (10.29), also mentions wives among those who are abandoned (18.29; 14.26). The history of the text, as in the parallels in Mark and Matthew, shows that at this point there has been a good deal of tinkering around, as if not all the tradents were sure whether the wife should be abandoned along with all the other members of the family. A comparative argument from the ascetical ethos of the Cynics, who had also chosen an itinerant form of life and mission, to the Jesus group, would suggest that they were unmarried, but this is not completely compelling; the two groups could have differed precisely on this point. The best evidence for leaving wives is in Luke. One could assume that he had inferred it from the Cynics whom he knew, whereas he came a generation after the group around Jesus.[205] The doyen of Protestant exegesis, Rudolf Bultmann, thought that Luke was simply more pedantic in his list than the other evangelists. The sources simply do not give us any clear information.

A series of other texts seem to tell more clearly against the possibility of the Jesus group being unmarried. The call to discipleship in Mark (10.29) has a continuation which is not in Matthew and Luke (10.30), where there is a list of what the itinerant preachers gain when they leave all, and not just in their earthly existence: houses, brothers, sisters, mothers, children (no fathers!) and fields a hundredfold. Anyone who leaves a house finds community with people of the same conviction in many houses. Anyone who leaves a physical family finds community with many people who attach themselves to the faith and so become sisters and mothers in the faith. As it is a sisterly community in which there is no domination, the authority of the father falls away. Was the wife left out in v.29 because otherwise the saying about reward in v.30 would have to say that the itinerant preachers would gain wives 'a hundredfold'?[206] Even this conclusion is not compelling, because the father was also left out in v.30 as opposed to v.29. So did the wives travel along, too?

The prohibition against putting away one's wife (Mark 10.11-12 par.; Mark 10.6-9) can hardly be cited in the case of the praxis of the Jesus group, as this text is not in the context of discipleship and is meant as an indictment of Jews who ask Jesus about a practice customary in Judaism.[207]

'Love' or asceticism?

A note in I Corinthians 9.5 perhaps brings us closer to a solution. This is the context: evidently Paul is accused by the community in Corinth of not being a real apostle (1-3). His renunciation of the claim of an apostle to be looked after by the community in order to earn his own living (cf. Acts 18.3) made the Corinthians doubt the legitimacy of his calling by the Lord (was he then still completely the servant of the gospel?). Paul, however, says that he is concerned not to be a burden on the community and bases his renunciation on his selfless devotion to the gospel (6 and 12). He then goes on to enumerate the privileges of the apostle, immediately stressing that he himself has never made use of them. Among other things he says: 'Have we not the right to take around a (Christian) sister as a wife (to see to the provisions of the community) like the other apostles and the brothers of the Lord and Cephas (Peter)?' According to this, Peter took his wife with him on his journeys and so the Jesus group were not celibates. It is interesting that about 150 years later Clement of Alexandria turns the phrase round: 'a wife like a (Christian) sister'.[208] In so doing he transforms the marriage of the followers of Jesus into a 'Joseph's marriage'.

This sentence is without doubt the strongest evidence that married men and their wives followed Jesus. As Paul knew Peter personally, the credibility of his statement is strengthened; but since, as I shall go on to demonstrate, there are some important arguments in favour of the view that members of the Jesus group were unmarried, we must attempt a cross-check. Paul mentions not only Peter but also the brothers of the Lord, whose names are given in Mark: James, Joses, Judas and Simon (6.3). Here, however, they appear in an unfavourable light as kinsfolk who take offence at Jesus. Later we find James as leader of the Christian community in Jerusalem, but it emerges from I Cor.15.7 that he joined the followers of Jesus only after Jesus' death. At least the brothers of the Lord did not travel around with Jesus himself. So the practice to which Paul refers seems to apply only to the time after the death of Jesus; at all events I Corinthians must have been written about twenty years after this event. This change can easily be explained in terms of the transformation of the radical ethos of the Jesus group in a slow adaptation to the pattern of life in local Christian communities. At the time of Paul both practices still existed side by side. There were itinerant missionaries, some still from the time of Jesus, and settled members of Christian communities. At the same time, married couples are mentioned, like Prisca and Aquila, who sometimes went with the itinerants – Prisca and Aquila joined Paul, sometimes gathered communities in their house and thus laid the basis for the local community. It would not be surprising if, for example, Peter and others following this pattern now also took their wives with them and wanted to put the burden of looking after them on the communities.

There are only a few texts to which those who want to demonstrate that Jesus and his followers lived a married life can refer. They are not clear enough. All arguments from them lack a compelling logic. Shalom Ben Chorin argues that because he was a Jew Jesus must have been married or widowed, since marriage and procreation were duties enjoined by religion.[209] But may Jesus be measured by the criteria of orthodox Judaism, when he differed from the tradition of his origin in so many respects and was subject to such vehement criticism? The question whether or not his followers were married can still most appropriately be answered from the self-understanding of the Jesus group. Now it is striking that in the subsequent generation marriage, love, children are not themes, in contrast, say, to Paul who is intensively occupied with such problems, at least in the communities (e.g. I Cor.7). The physical family is put at a distance, and the 'praise of castration' (Matt.19.12) is not supporting evidence for a positive attitude to marriage.[210] What led Jesus and his followers to choose so radical a life-style which so conflicted with the usual social forms?

The group was moved by the conviction that the kingdom of God would come soon. That goes against all that is valid 'in the world'. It represents a new 'order', which is lived out predominantly in the Jesus group; there is no illness, no hunger, no thirst in the community of brothers and sisters who are not defined in physical terms; all share everything, no one rules over the others; men do not even rule over women, but all serve one another. In normal circumstances such a claim cannot be realized, therefore those convinced of the coming of the kingdom of God leave their normal modes of life and travel around homeless and without possessions, with the aim of gathering and assembling those of like mind. And in this situation is the shared life of men and women in marriage, which has been so fraught through history, going to be maintained? At all events, this argument seems to me more probable than all the arguments that marriage was practised in the Jesus group.

At that time, for a Jew not infected by Hellenistic *laissez-faire*, marriage always also meant children. If the kingdom of God overcomes the conditions of the finite world, then all the tribulation that women have in marriage, in having children and bringing them up, will be rewarded. And finally the kingdom of God is also expected soon; so is it worth while continuing to bring children into this world in order to hand them over to the suffering in which everything will soon come to an end? What motivates Paul himself not to be married and also to commend this form of life is all the more valid for the radical followers of Jesus (I Cor.7.28-29). Conversion always also means turning away from what is important to the world. The situation of a group which expresses a very decided conviction gives clearer information than isolated texts. That should be remembered so that wishful thinking does not identify friendship with sexual intercourse and people do not, like Elisabeth Moltmann-Wendel, argue imaginatively from familiarity to eroticism.[211] Those with and around Jesus are familiar friends as '*familia Dei*'.[212]

One of the problems of our day is that we are terrified by the word asceticism – which is what the group of radical itinerant preachers is all about – because behind it we feel repression which is a threat to life, anxiety about contact, about being seized by something which puts us at its disposal. Images of staining and impurity play a role. This form of asceticism also has a tradition; for example it lies behind the ritual purity laws of the Old Testament tradition. Anxiety over tabu[213] produces the idea that sexuality, fertility, blood, women are 'powers' which have to be banished. Not a trace of such motives can be found in the Jesus tradition. On the contrary, Jesus constantly attacks this ritual ideal of purity by contrasting with it the 'ethical' purity of the heart (e.g. Mark 7.14ff.; Matt.12.1ff.; Matt.23.25-27). When Jesus touches the woman 'with an issue of blood' (i.e. who menstruates constantly) or is touched by her, he shows his contempt for tabu asceticism. According to the law of purity this would have made Jesus unclean; he should have avoided all human contact and not allowed himself to be touched until the purification rites had been performed. He should have reprimanded the woman because she knew what contact with her meant for him. Jesus did nothing of the sort; he let himself be touched and was seized with pity; for this woman had not only already suffered from the illness for many years, but in addition had been leading the life of an outcast from human society for the same period (cf. Lev.15.19ff.; 12.1ff.). Being healed and blessing are Jesus' answer to the breaking of a tabu.

The asceticism of the Jesus group has another, positive intention. It becomes understandable against the background of Jewish life in the first century which could be extremely humiliating and even a threat to existence and which could seem no longer capable of being reconciled to the saving will of God. Departure from the network of social conditioning at the time is not to be seen as a flight from responsibility; it means leaving behind a corrupt world, far removed from the will of God in its guilt. This was to be renewed through the call to repentance, not through measures of social reform but through a change in the attitude of human beings. In view of this, emphases shifted. Should one bring up children and look after house and land where sowing and harvesting were inappropriate? The connection between sexuality, descendants and the concerns which arise from them will have been more obvious then than now, when we can avoid some of them by contraception, the romanticism of 'being a couple' and the Enlightenment postulate of the 'right to...' can relieve us of some of them; and some of the unavoidable tribulations are recognized too late. Sexuality with all its consequences becomes a particular burden when there is no longer an answer to the question of one's daily bread.

Asceticism motivated by a hope for the coming kingdom of God and the reversal of all customary earthly values brings liberation. Much that causes trouble becomes insignificant. The longing for an abolition of the sorry conditions of an earthly existence leaves behind what has become intolerable even now, and not just at the end of the day. In the face of the kingdom of God and its perfection one's gaze is sharpened for the limitations of the earthly: if in the kingdom of God there is no suffering, no ruling over people, no hunger and ultimately no more death because only that dies which is hostile to humanity, then we should end our ties to what is hostile to us, to house, family and possessions. This belief of Jesus and his followers is borne up by trust in the one God who is good to us and will free us from our burdens – like the lilies of the field... Besides, this 'model' also indicates the significance of – voluntary – celibacy.

This belief in the coming of the kingdom of God makes it extremely probable that as well as being homeless and without possessions the group around Jesus were also unmarried. The practice of so-called 'free love' in which fantasies always involve Jesus and Mary Magdalene remain sheer speculation. As the geographical area which the itinerant preachers covered was not great, there will certainly have been further contacts with the families who stayed where they were (as in the case of Peter), provided that these families did not take offence, as they did in Jesus' own case.

After the death of Jesus and in the course of the transition to the formation of settled local communities we find married couples who are expressly mentioned by name; these no longer travelled around as itinerant preachers in the same radical way but travelled, and then remained for some length of time in one place, in order to make the Christians in their own house into a community. Such house communities then turned into local communities. Apostles from the circle around Jesus who were still alive at that time then evidently fell in with this practice and took their wives travelling with them. Since by this time, e.g. about twenty years after the death of Jesus, there were already a large number of Christian communities, the praxis of the radical itinerant preachers also changed to the practice of the travelling missionaries, in which the missionaries could rely on fixed bases. That made it easier for them to take wives and possibly children with them. Just as, for example, the brothers of Jesus attached themselves to Christian faith only after the death of Jesus as a result of appearances of the risen Christ, so too some wives of the apostles could have been converted, especially as the radical ethos had become milder. At any rate one thing was certain: the wife had to be a sister in the faith. The principle of inclusiveness remained valid.

The significance of this situation in detail must remain open. Had the ascetical claim established itself so much at that time that the wives indeed travelled with their husbands but did not have sexual intercourse with them (cf. I Cor.7.29)? As there were now communities to provide care in place of the original family, perhaps this particular motive led to wives being taken along. Be this as it may, in I Corinthians 9.5 there is mention only of care.

The number of women among the Christians seems to have increased considerably as a result of the formation of communities. Only now do we find the mother of Jesus among his followers (Acts 1.14). This gave rise to problems which are not mentioned in the group around Jesus because they do not concern the unmarried. The entry into the community of women as wives and mothers also changed the estimation of them, as is evident from the texts of the third generation. We shall come back to them later.

CHAPTER FOUR

At the Foot of the Cross

Social and political conditions

In this chapter, too, I am concerned with sketching out the circumstances of New Testament times and thus avoiding over-hasty identifications with men and women in the biblical texts. The praxis of a faith is historically determined and each generation must ask afresh how its praxis may look in the context of the circumstances of the age. So a naive transference from then to now is not possible.

In order to describe circumstances I am again going back to taxes. In addition to political taxes there were religious offerings which had to be made in the Jerusalem temple. The temple was not just a religious centre but an economic centre, comparable to a bank. Its income consisted of offerings required by the law, the Torah, of gifts, income through the sacrificial trade and of proceeds of all the businesses which cluster round a place of pilgrimage. Where faith was counted for something and a Jew's conscience obliged him to act in accordance with his financial circumstances, the expense could be quite considerable.

First there was the gift of firstfruits, a particular part of the harvest of corn, wine, oil and other agricultural products. This offering of the firstfruits was holy and was eaten by the temple priests in a state of cultic purity. The level of the offering varied considerably: from 1% to 30% (according to the school of Shammai) or 40% (thus according to the school of Hillel); and as one could adapt it to social conditions, this demand for tax was usally met. Even the 'am-ha-arets, the group of Jews suspected of having a pagan disposition, observed the offering of firstfruits.

Then came the first tithe to the Levites, who in turn passed on a tenth to the priests, and the second tithe, which to begin with remained in the possession of the owner, to be taken up on the occasion of the next pilgrimage to Jerusalem and to be eaten there. Since many Jews at that time lived in the Diaspora and had limited possibilities of travelling up to Jerusalem, they were allowed to sell the second tithe and use the proceeds for their next pilgrimage. They could then buy the food they needed for the cultic meal when they arrived. What was not spent was given to the poor.

A fourth offering was the tithe for the poor. This requirement was least observed, as there was least pressure behind it. Only those who took the law very seriously, like the Pharisees, observed it.

It is evident that the poor smallholders were most deeply affected by such an abundance of taxes. It was without doubt most difficult of all to observe the regulations for the sabbath year: in the seventh year it was unlawful to plant or reap or – in the case of fruit trees – prune. It was not even permissible to eat what ripened of itself in the seventh year. The result of the prohibition on a harvest in the seventh year was that one could neither plough nor sow even in the sixth year. Whereas the diaspora Jews were still prepared to pay the offering of first fruits or the tithes, they refrained from observing the sabbath year, since this regulation brought insuperable burdens, particularly on the poorer farmers. Anyone who observed the sabbath year had to have sufficient in store to be able to do so. We can see something of these burdens from, for example, regulations about the wild endive. Normally it was not eaten, but it was during the sabbath year. In the theatre at Caesarea the public amused themselves by mocking the Jewish endive eaters.[214]

The social situation had an effect on matters of faith. The religious taxes swallowed up enormous sums if they were really observed by a pious Jew. Again it was the poor in particular who had most to suffer under the conflict. They were confronted with the alternative of observing the religious commandment and going hungry or breaking the commandment in order to survive and becoming sinners. The religious significance of these offerings originally lay in their intent to remind people that all that the earth produces comes from God's hand: freely one receives, therefore one must give freely. Poverty now completely reversed the good intentions of the law. A reality which threatened life could no longer put into effect the good intention of the Torah, which sought to serve life. God's good law turned against people. The God of the Torah became an enemy of the poor; those among the poor who observed the law began to feel an inhumanity which had not been intended. Only the rich were in the favourable position of being able to observe the law of God and thus count themselves among the righteous. But they often no longer had the intention of being pious; at most they wanted to appear pious.

This sheds a new life on what the New Testament understands a sinner, a law-breaker to be, and it sheds new life on the law itself. The further the distance from the cult centre of Jerusalem, the less the law applied; detachment was easier, and both sin and the Law lost significance. The forms in which faith was expressed were in conflict with everyday existence. Those who, like the Pharisees, not only observed the law but wanted to help towards renewing it to the best of their ability, yet did not see that reality itself had perverted God's good law into its opposite, could no longer be regarded as interpreters of God's will by those who were affected by it. Jesus recognized the loss of humanity in the law and gave expression to it. The law, the sabbath is there for human beings and not *vice versa* (Mark 2.27). Sinners and publicans, poor and sick, are combinations which are often repeated in the New Testament. Only the kingdom of God gives them a possibility of life. Jesus's dealings with those who are despised by the law stamp his career and make it particularly offensive to the pious. Sinners who cannot stand before the severe demands of the law will probably also have learnt vice by necessity, and the poor had nothing out of which they could give God and the needy their share. Nowadays we may understand sin as referring to misdeeds in sexual matters, but that is by no means all that had become a problem in Palestine in the first century. The prostitutes are also to be seen in this context, since for many women the 'oldest profession' was the only chance of survival.

Such social conditions did not just undermine the authority of the law but did so decisively, so that another criterion proved necessary: the good is what brings salvation to human beings. So Jesus' call to a change of heart alters the hierarchy of values: compassion, being affected by the suffering of others, has an advantage over righteousness. How offensive such an attitude is, emerges from the defensiveness which is a direct reaction even today to the parable of the workers in the vineyard (Matt.20.1ff.); I have felt it time and again in my work as a mediator. The gift of the owner of the vineyard to the day labourers, the poor, is more than a fair wage. 'In the Jesus movement the tremendous insight dawned that solidarity is more than morality.'[215] The people whom Jesus met were no longer defined in terms of current ethical and religious norms – not even women, to whom the claim of the norm applied to an intensified degree at all times. For Jesus everyone, men included, is in need of redemption. Along with the normative validity of what is intended to be the good law of God, the double morality in assessing the action of men and women also disappears. That is the theological background to all the passages in the New Testament which are about dealings with sinners, men and women. For the secular world of values was in a crisis.

It would be inappropriate to accuse Judaism as a whole of legalism in the sense of a formal fulfilment of the law without honest demands on the conscience, as often happens. The degree to which a distinction was also made in the Jewish tradition between heteronomous, external morality and autonomous morality accepted inwardly is shown above all by prophetic criticism. By contrast Jesus responds to a much more fundamental questioning of traditional norms which could no longer cope with the changed realities of life. But that in turn also raises the basic problem of all ethics: that being able to distinguish between good and evil and thus to know what good is does not necessarily also mean being able to do the good – and that applies to men and women equally. In this interpretation of Genesis 3 men and women participate equally in fallen creation, and both are in need of redeeming forgiveness.

The courage of devotion

A further aspect can be noted in the question of the religious and social significance of the Jerusalem temple. The priestly nobility, the Sadducees, on the one hand were still among the religious élite, though they had long since been corrupted. Their position was due not least to their economic interests, since the temple had immense incomes: its taxes, gifts, and lands were capable not only of financing the rebuilding (from 20 BC to about AD 60) but also of feeding the whole priesthood. And there was enough after that to be hoarded in the temple treasury. The fact that the high priests and their families did not shrink from getting their share by force and kept the priests to the lower ranks of the hierarchy shows how little the self-understanding of this 'élite' was governed by religious motives. Thus for example it is reported:

> Now with each passing day the (former) high priest Ananias rose in the esteem of the people and became increasingly honoured and revered. He was very able in financial affairs and managed to sway both Albinus the governor and the high priest with bribes. But he had good-for-nothing servants who came to an arrangement with rogues to plunder the threshing floors of the tithes belonging to the priests and anyone who ventured to resist them was beaten and ill-treated. The high priests used servants in the same way as Ananias, and as no one could withstand them, the priests inevitably perished of hunger, since they lived off the tithes.[216]

This text of Josephus also gives us some indication of how easy it was to blind 'the people' by appearances.[217] Josephus also tells us that the priests often helped at the harvest in order to be able to get their share straight away. This, however, was no longer regarded in the religious sense as a tithe but was declared profane, and thus simply served to ensure their survival.[218]

Secondly, the political situation also called for a balance of power interests. Apart from occasional interventions, the Romans respected Jewish worship. They left the temple treasure untouched and did not compel the Jews to offer emperor worship. Nevertheless the Jerusalem cult community had no autonomy. At the time of Herod the Great it was dependent on the king, who had the position of an ally of Rome and was responsible directly to the Roman senate. Herod nominated the high priest at will. Once Judaea had become a procuratorial province, the Romans themselves appointed the high priests, so that both sides were primarily concerned for political equilibrium. Then began the usual political battle or tactical manoeuvring over who could secure advantages and avoid disadvantages and how. Rome was not unimpressed by the religious and economic power of the temple: the procurators must have been concerned to avoid rebellions and quieten down crisis spots, as they had to answer to the Emperor in Rome. That is the only way of understanding why the Jewish Sanhedrin, the court of justice, could press Pontius Pilate to condemn and execute Jesus (John 19.8,12,15).

Conversely the Jews were afraid of the military strength of Rome and the extraction of taxes, and the high priests were above all afraid of losing face before the people as collaborators, which is what they were. That would not least have had an effect on income. Such mutual anxieties produced an equilibrium of terror which threatened to get out of control, now in favour of one side and now in favour of the other. At all events Rome had all the leverage, as is evident from the fate of Jerusalem. That the temple hierarchy was open to corruption is understandable at least from the political situation, as such pressure does not exactly favour the development of integrity in matters of faith. The criticism of the people, above all outside Jerusalem (cf. John 7.41,52), provided the answer. In his preaching of judgment John the Baptist already called for repentance and referred to the Sadducees as a brood of serpents (Matt.3.7f.).

The critical words of Jesus against the temple and his prophetic anger against those who bought and sold and changed money in the temple forecourt also belong in this context. Here he links up with the prophetic tradition which centuries before had contrasted an honest attitude of faith with what went on in the temple. Jesus' actions must also have alarmed the hierarchy, particularly if this criticism was also bound up with a messianic claim.[219] By going to Jerusalem, the hated city, and preaching the kingdom of God in the temple, 'the lions' den', Jesus could expect counter measures and will probably also have been aware of this. Without doubt the Sadducees had an interest in silencing this warning voice which destroyed the appearances they had created laboriously and at considerable financial expense.

As a result of a fear of rebellion the Sanhedrin had on its side the procurator Pontius Pilate, who had killed more than one person for the sake of his political career. The collaboration also worked in this case, for the two power blocks were not interested in criticism. At any rate that was the decisive reason, for they certainly did not understand the significance of the preaching of the kingdom of God. The crucifixion to which Jesus was condemned was the usual form of execution for enemies of the Roman state. Thousands died this death before and after Jesus, above all the Zealots. The torment which was associated with death on the cross was regarded as heightened punishment for 'elements disruptive to the state'. In addition the dead man was refused a burial in accordance with piety: the birds of the air were to devour the corpses. The remains were put in a mass grave. That is why the Roman soldiers had to keep watch. They were to prevent friends or relatives stealing the body, to pay last respects to the dead.

Moreover it was dangerous for members of the family to make themselves known as such. The Romans did not hesitate to inflict the same death on relatives or followers of an enemy of the state. That also applied to wives and children. So Peter's denial can also be understood from this political aspect and may not be interpreted just as an individual personal failure. Even lamentation over the executed person was forbidden: 'Nor was it permitted to relatives or friends to stand near, to weep over them, or even to view them too long, but a cordon of sentries, with eyes for each beholder's sorrow, escorted the rotting carcasses.'[220]

In view of the dangers of such an undertaking it was a particular expression of courage that 'many women', including Mary from Magdala, Mary the mother of James, the mother of Joses and Salome (Mark 15.40f.par.) looked on 'from afar'. Only the independent christological interest of a later time also put Mary, the mother of Jesus, under the cross (John 19.25-27) to show that Jesus, the true God of the Christian confession, is wholly true man, born of a woman, and died under Pontius Pilate. Mary Magdalene indisputably stands in first place, and she is also among the women who go to the tomb on Easter morning. To be seen by the grave of an enemy of the state was just as risky as being found in the proximity of the cross. As a result of political intervention – he was a respected member of a 'council', we do not know which – Joseph of Arimathea managed to get the body of Jesus, to preserve it from the mass grave and anonymity. Nevertheless the anxiety that the tombs of enemies of state could become places of pilgrimage existed, and as a result the women by the grave were putting themselves in danger by wanting to pay the dead body the honour due in piety. The rest of the followers had run away and were in hiding in Jerusalem.

To begin with, neither the disciples nor the women disciples believed in a resurrection. By wanting to anoint the body the women at the same time indicated that they regarded Jesus as dead.[221] So they had no more faith than the men, and therefore the angel is also chiding them when he asks why they seek the living among the dead (Luke 24.5). They are not, however, put off by the danger which their action represents, and so become the first recipients of the Easter message, and at the same time are charged with handing it on.

It is to the credit of feminist theology that through its interest and exegetical accuracy it has made us aware of something that exegetes have not seen or have not even wanted to see. Thus for example the doyen of Protestant exegesis, Rudolf Bultmann, declared that the women under the cross were an 'isolated piece of tradition':[222] 'As at the Resurrection, women are here named as witnesses. They are not historical in either place.'[223] The reader is not given any reason for this exegetical judgment. Other exegetes want to see these verses as a redactional composition of the evangelist and so reject their historical authenticity. Today we look critically on such attempts: there are 'no convincing literary-critical arguments for assigning the lists (he means the lists of women's names) to different levels or strata of the tradition... All attempts to declare one or more lists in turn, in various groupings, as redactional compositions, completely disregard the question of historical tradition and burden the assumed redactors with the composition of arbitrary lists – an unprecedented occurrence as long as the motivation and result of the alleged reactions are not plausibly explained.'[224] Not least this verdict also shows the stubbornness of an interest in making women disappear. So can the verdict of Rudolf Bultmann be based on anything other than such an interest?

Women in the Jesus tradition

As a result of concealed references that have been brought to light again we can finally sketch out something of the significance of the women around Jesus. These are references which delight those who are concerned for a peaceful and balanced relationship between the sexes.

1. Women, some of them mentioned by name, were as much followers of Jesus as men were, as were the 'twelve apostles' that history has created. The criterion that was of such decisive significance for the Jesus group applied to both women and men: personal decision, following the call to repentance. The conviction of the coming of the kingdom of God in the face of which all the kingdoms of this world represent an anti-kingdom was matched by a credible and uncompromising praxis: no possessions, no firm abode; instead complete commitment to the realization and proclamation of this conviction. The individual, whether male or female, was judged by nothing other than faith. Women and men live out the exodus.

2. Tabu conceptions in accordance with the cultic ideal of purity (fertility, blood) which have so far provoked anxiety and repudiation do not hold, but are criticized and done away with. The debate over the ordination of women in the churches of the Reformation during the 1960s has shown that such conceptions, although they are not an official argument, are very much alive. Over against this, Jesus again regards, or turns to, the person capable of decision, as is shown by the pericope about the woman with an issue of blood; he considers the individual who suffers, whether man or woman.

3. In the group around Jesus all human beings are regarded as fallible and in need of redemption, women no more than men. It is not the current morality which is decisive in judging action, nor is there a double morality, i.e. a morality for men and a morality for women. With Jesus, compassion and a concern for change relate to both sexes.

4. For a long time courage has been regarded as a cardinal male virtue, and this can be attested not least in the definition of the animus in the work of Jung. The passion narrative shows that women are not interpreted in terms of the cliché of anxiety, and

the texts hand down the courage that they in fact showed. As a result the women are the first to receive the epiphany and the charge to proclaim the Easter message.

5. Among the followers of Jesus the renunciation of any form of the exercise of power is called for not only from women but also particularly from men. All are called on to serve one another. The community is one of brothers and sisters: rank and status are transcended. The passion of Jesus, the passion of a man, shows the consequences of such a claim.

6. Jesus and his followers, men and women, leave the usual social ties, which primarily include the family. As a result the controversy over the question whether the woman's place is not in the home proves superfluous.

7. If we begin from the practice of celibacy or at least its higher evaluation, which seems plausible given the situation in which the group around Jesus lived and its values, the problem of eroticism, desire and the consequences from which women suffer when they are regarded one-sidedly as the object of such desire, proves superfluous.

What has been said on points 1 to 5 represents an enormous shift in criteria over against the praxis, and the theory which goes with it, which holds even today and even in Christian communities. If one thinks in terms of the circumstances of the Jesus group, however, some major doubts arise as to whether these criteria can be transferred so easily into another context. What about women find themselves who do not travel but live at home? Who cannot be without possessions because they have children to look after? Who do not want to or cannot avoid the power of eros – and that is the presupposition of what has just been said? The radical ethics of the itinerant preachers for the sake of the kingdom of God calls for an exodus from the ties which women mostly make. It will also emerge that the change in life-style as a result of the formation of stable local communities also changed the estimation of women and the sphere of their activity. The call to mission which detaches people from their ordinary social context by calling them to discipleship becomes a mission command aimed at forming a community and thus requires fixed social forms, i.e. the family (house community).

Here we come upon a discovery which already emerged from

the contrast between Tertullian and Clement of Alexandria: the equal estimation of women as people who are capable of decision and conviction, fellow-Christians and witnesses to the gospel, is combined with a radical ethos, a subversive practice and a basic ascetical attitude. Where women are in the context of their families, the balance shifts against them and all the arguments emerge again which the preaching of the kingdom of God had made superfluous: their place in the home, their exclusion from public life, their lack of conviction, anxiety at the power of love and fertility, a double moral standard, anxiety, subordination to the power of authorities.

CHAPTER FIVE

Paul the Scapegoat

In feminist literature Paul is also clearly the most attacked person in the New Testament: he has been made responsible for all the misfortunes of a Christian tradition which is hostile to women and indeed leads to neurosis.[225] Unconcealed hatred is directed against Paul, as it is against the church fathers. Does a reading of the Pauline texts confirm the justification for such hatred, or is this not rather the result of questionable exegesis of Paul in schools and from pulpits? In order to be able to answer the question, we again need to make a number of distinctions. First, a distinction must be made between the person of Paul and the situation of the community in which he finds himself or with which he argues. The conviction and praxis of the early Christian communities are not necessarily identical with those of Paul; in the end there were also conflicts between them. Secondly, a distinction must be made between traditional material and the interests of the time. Thirdly, a distinction must be made between the authentic Pauline letters and the 'letters' which are attributed to Paul but which do not come from him. It is striking that Roman Catholic feminist literature in particular pays little heed to such a distinction or does not attach any significance to it.[226] But it has precisely that in common with the practice of the churches in teaching and preaching. Therefore, fourthly, present practice in communication must also be measured by the criterion of historical-critical work and in that way a distinction be made between the present interest of the churches and the intention of the New Testament writings. As the history of his influence shows, Paul is also responsible for legitimating a good deal of wishful thinking.

Lydia and the godfearers

It was women in particular who felt particularly attracted by the Christian missionaries. The reasons for this can be demonstrated from the formation of the community in Philippi.[227] In Acts 16.12f. it is reported that Paul and Timothy travelled to Macedonia and to Philippi on the basis of a nocturnal vision. Philippi was a colony, which meant that it was mainly settled by soldiers who had retired from service for Rome. Presumably Philippi did not have a synagogue, for otherwise Paul would have sought it out, as was his custom, to preach there. Instead there was a Jewish place of prayer outside the city gate where women assembled. According to Jewish law at least ten Jewish men were needed to found a synagogue; women could not found one. So evidently there were only a few Jews in Philippi, at any rate less than ten men and some women.

On the sabbath, Acts continues (v.13), Paul and Timothy went to the place of prayer by the river where the women had gathered. These included Lydia, a dealer in purple, from Thyatira (v.14). She was not a Jew but a 'godfearer'. The translations speak of a godfearing woman, which a naive reading would understand as a 'pious' woman. However, the godfearers were not just pious people but Gentiles who were attached to Judaism without being numbered among the proselytes, those who were fully converted to Jewish faith. So behind this word as a technical term is a clearly defined form of faith and life. Anyone who was a godfearer above all observed the ethical instructions, the Torah, of the Jews, and also went to synagogue worship (where there was a synagogue), or as in the case of Lydia took part in common prayer: however, men did not undergo circumcision or the baptism provided for full proselytes. The godfearers already made a close link between Gentiles and Jews before the Christian mission to the Gentiles.

A further important element is to be noted in connection with the godfearers. Strikingly enough, pagan women in particular tended to become godfearers. The following account by Josephus may illuminate the reason why.[228] During the Jewish war, in 66, the Roman consul Cestius was drawn into the difficulties which the procurator of Judaea, Gessius Florus, had got into with rebel Zealots. Thereupon Cestius besieged Jerusalem, but had to withdraw without any success. The waging of the war was then handed over to Vespasian, and Cestius attempted to justify himself to Nero, who was emperor at the time, by putting the blame on Florus. In this connection Josephus goes on to report that the inhabitants of Damascus heard of the discomfiture of the Romans and wanted to kill a large number of Jews whom they had taken prisoner and shut up in a gymnasium. 'Only they were afraid of their own wives, as almost without exception they belonged to the Jewish religion. So they asked them all to conceal their intention from their wives.'[229] After that they slaughtered the defenceless Jews – 10,500 people in an hour.

It seems plausible from this story why these pagan women felt attracted by the Jewish faith and particularly by the ethical implications of the law. The longer it went on, the more the immense brutality of a political system which so blatantly cherished power and strength, and domination of some human beings by others, as its ideal and put it into action, called for an alternative.

The Lydia of Acts was a well-to-do woman, for dealing in purple was regarded as a profitable business. So she must also have had some independence. Enthused by Paul's sermon, she was baptized and her whole house with her. This house community of Lydia's was the cradle of the Christian community in Philippi.

The 'case' of Lydia is symptomatic, for she was not the only one among the godfearers who took this course.[230] The opening up of the Christian mission to Gentiles resulted in the surrender of many Jewish elements which were impossible for godfearers: circumcision, the observance of ritual laws and the strict observance of the precepts of the law expounded casuistically by the Jewish scribes. Therefore women like Lydia must have found Christian faith even better and more in accord with their hopes.

In addition, the Christian confession brought a conversion in that estimation of women which was current both in Judaism and among the Gentiles. The well-known and already often cited text from Gal. 3.28 is a primitive Christian baptismal formula which is taken over and quoted by Paul: 'For as many of you as were baptized into Christ have put on Christ. There is neither Jew nor Greek, there is neither slave nor free, there is neither male nor female, for you are all one in Christ Jesus.'[231] This formula declares that the classical human points of conflict – ethnic differences, social status and the sex war, all fields of tension which were a particular occasion for the formation of prejudice and discriminatory behaviour – are irrelevant to the Christian community.

Community life in the Christian community was thus regulated by criteria which went against the criteria customary elsewhere in the world. The Hellenistic man had three reasons to be grateful: first, that he had been born a man and not an animal; secondly, that he had been born a man and not a woman; and thirdly, that he was a Greek and not a barbarian.[232] With some variants a Jew, too, had reason to be glad: 'A person must say three praises a day: Praised be Thou who hast not made me a Gentile, praised be Thou who hast not made me a woman, praised be Thou who has not made me a slave.'[233] Much as these men differ in ethnic character, they are united in gratitude that they have the 'right' sex. 'But it must not be like this among you' (Mark 10.43) runs the Christian answer.

The reversal of values expressed by the baptismal formula in Galatians is very closely connected with the Jesus tradition. Not only the itinerant preachers but also Christians in a settled community committed themselves to the criteria of the kingdom of God that Jesus had preached, for in the last resort they were convinced that as the Risen One the Lord was alive and at work among them. In commentaries on Gal.3.28 one keeps reading that this is an eschatological hope which will only materialize at the 'end of days' when God creates a new heaven and a new earth; here and now things remain as they were.[234] Some exegetes also distinguish a saving significance 'before God', which has no significance 'before men'. This is first contradicted by the context, which is concerned with baptism, with fellowship with Christ and thus with the community, concerned to arrange its praxis in accordance with the Spirit of Christ (cf. I Cor.12.1ff.). Through baptism a person is already made new here and now by putting on Christ. The experience that the claim of Gal.3.28 was not always realized does not do away with the claim, and anyone who argues that this applies only to 'the end of the days' and is valid only 'before God' leaves reality to its own laws. That would make the Christian community just the same as any other gathering of people, and the significance of being 'in Christ' would be limited to the hope that this world might end as soon as possible. However, that goes against the self-understanding of the Christian community which is attested in the New Testament and specifically also in Paul, namely that the community is the anticipation of what is to apply to the whole world at the end of days: no suffering, no death, no discrimination. The community as the body of Christ is a pledge, an advance, an image of the heavenly perfection (cf. e.g. Rom.8.23,30; II Cor.1.22; 3.16-18; 4.10-12; 5.5; Eph.1.14).

As long as the community of Christ lives in the world, it is in conflict with the powers which do not share its conviction. Such a combat would be superfluous if Christians merely had another theory to offer. A claim becomes dangerous only when it is matched by a praxis, and in fact there is historical evidence for the realization of 'there is neither man nor woman' in the communities in the time of Paul.

Women, tasks and ministries

The special significance of women for the spread of Christian faith in the first century and beyond has been stressed in many exegetical works since the beginning of our century. But evidently here, too, it was feminist interest that saw to it that a wider public could become aware of the fact.[235] Nevertheless the most important persons and texts need to be presented. Paul did not found personally all the communities of which we hear, as he did that at Philippi. He could rely on already existing communities as bases for his journeys. Moreover, many women whom he mentions as his fellow workers had not become Christians as a result of him. When Paul appeared, there was already a series of communities, like that in Rome, and Paul met women of acknowledged status who were actively engaged in mission and the building up of the community independently of him. To do Paul justice, one must first see and recognize that not only does he nowhere question working with these women but he confirms, values and at times stresses it – more often and more explicitly than any other author in the New Testament. And this is evidence of something else, namely that at this time women had an undeniable and unmistakable significance.

About a quarter of the active collaborators mentioned by name in the letters of Paul are women. If we add Nympha, mentioned in Colossians, the Pauline authorship of which is disputed, that gives us eleven of them. In alphabetical order these are Euodia, Julia, Junia, Mary, Nympha, Persis, Phoebe, Prisca, Syntyche, Tryphaena and Tryphosa. Most of them appear in the long list of greetings at the end of Romans (16.1-16): Junia and her husband Andronicus do not in any way fall short of the apostle Paul: similarly Jews, they had become Christians before him. It is also said that they have been in prison with Paul. Not only are they regarded as apostles, as Paul is, but they are also singled out as being 'preeminent' among the apostles. We do not hear more about Junia. There is only a bare mention of Julia and her husband Philologus, so they are a secondary missionary couple. Mary, the 'beloved' Persis, Tryphaena and Tryphosa have worked hard 'in (the service of) the Lord' and 'given their utmost'. The mother of Rufus and the sister of Nereus remain anonymous.

There is an at first somewhat disparaging mention of Euodia and Syntyche in Philippians. They are admonished by Paul to be 'in harmony in the Lord' (4.2f.). It can be concluded from this that they had been at odds.[236] They must have been respected women among the leaders of the community, for Paul calls them not only fellow workers, but fellow fighters in the Gospel (cf.1.27), in other words missionaries. Paul does not blame them for the dispute but wants to see that unity is restored. Nor does the dispute in any way damage the services of the two women, since it is said that their names stand in the 'Book of Life', in which proven and steadfast martyrs are entered (cf. Rev.3.5). So Euodia and Syntyche had at least suffered persecutions like Paul and other fellow fighters. Whether they were fellow prisoners with him like Junia and Andronicus does not emerge with certainty from the short text, but there is a good deal of probability that they were. It remains unclear over what the two women were in disagreement,[237] but just these two verses give a realistic and honest scene without idealizations: women and men, equally tested in missionary and community leadership, equally affected by persecutions, and finally equally not completely in agreement between themselves (cf. the dispute among the men in I Cor.3.1ff.). We can even be grateful that the women were at odds, for otherwise tradition would have been silent about the significant women in the Book of Life.

We meet Nympha in Col.4.15: 'Greet the brothers in Laodicea and Nympha and the community in her house.' Like for example Priscilla or Lydia, Nympha was the leader of her own house community; the history of the text is interesting at this point: some later tradents changed Nympha into a male Nymphas.[238]

Alongside Prisca, who has already been portrayed,[239] Phoebe still stands out especially (Rom.16.1). She is a deacon of the community in Cenchreae, the eastern harbour of Corinth, from which people sailed in the direction of Asia Minor. As Paul also sends special greetings to the *episcopoi*, the presidents of the council of elders, and the deacons, alongside all the other Christians in Philippi (Phil.1.1), these must be designations of office.[240] Paul can also use the term *diakonos*, servant, in other contexts quite generally to denote service in the gospel, and this causes many commentators to see Phoebe simply as a Christian woman. However, in Rom.16.1 the word deacon seems clearly to be stressed in connection with the mention of the community (*ekklesia*). Phoebe is referred to with the masculine 'deacon', from which it emerges that at that time there was no distinction between a male deacon and a female deacon.[241]

The underlying interest behind the concern of feminists today to feminize designations of function or titles of office is clear and understandable. Experience shows that when confronted with more senior titles people automatically assume that the person concerned is a man, even if a clearly feminine first name follows. I myself have a nice collection of letters addressed to 'Herr Professor Dr Susanne Heine'. But prejudices go deep. Anyone who, whether consciously or unconsciously, does not want to have women in senior office and functions, tends not only to overlook feminine first names but also to belittle the office when it is held by a woman. The social prestige of a function in society is closely connected with the social prestige of the group concerned. When women are belittled, their 'ministry' also loses respect. A deaconess today is quite different from a deacon in the church hierarchy. If one were to speak of Phoebe the deaconess people would tend to think of some function in charitable service at the lower end of the career ladder. We should at least be aware of this negative effect of the feminization of titles of office.

Romans 16 is a letter of commendation for Phoebe, who evidently wants to travel to Rome (or, more probably, to Ephesus, for this chapter is out of context in the general setting of Romans).[242] So like other women, e.g. Prisca, she travels. Paul asks the community to support her in all things, 'for she too has been a *prostasis* to many, including myself' (v.2). The term *prostasis* is much disputed and will probably never be clarified completely. It can mean both helper and support and also community leader, president. As Phoebe is a woman, most commentators have spoken of 'personal care'[243] – but nothing public! Two textual passages which use the same Greek word as a verb, Rom.12.8; I Thess.5.12, suggest that we should regard Phoebe, too, as holding a leading function in the community.[244] According to I Thess.5.12 it is the task of the leader of the community to admonish the community. When Paul says that Phoebe has also been a *prostasis* to him, one might think that she had had occasion to admonish him.

A short look at Acts increases our list of women's names: Mary the mother of John Mark is in charge of a house community in Jerusalem which also includes the maid Rhoda (12.12,13). The obviously prosperous Tabitha in Joppa, a 'disciple', makes clothes for widows, is full of good works and almsgiving, and is restored to life by Peter after being carried off by an illness (9.36ff.). Damaris in Athens is converted by Paul's preaching (17.34) and the 'evangelist' Philip in Caesarea had four virgin daughters who were active as prophetesses (21.9). And finally, Mary the mother of Jesus is among the assembled Christians in the community in Jerusalem (1.14).

Not all Christians were or remained orthodox at that time. A number of false prophets disturbed the communities, as did some false prophetesses, like the Jezebel mentioned in Revelation (2.20ff.).

Despite the none too lavish sources, we can reconstruct a vivid picture of community life at the time and the women involved: their influence extended from Caesarea to Rome. Mothers, wives, sisters (in this case physical and not just Christian sisters) and young girls worked at spreading the new faith and building up the communities. Their functions ranged from the highest to the 'lowest'. They worked as apostles, deacons, community leaders, teachers and prophets. They travelled as missionaries and did charitable work; they preached, taught, gathered the believers together and sewed clothes for women. There were well-to-do women among them who shared what they had and kept open house, and there were poor women and slaves. They worked hard, had their differences of opinion, and could be bewitched by heretical teachers. In all this they were no different from men and fellow Christians. Consequently one can only find the verdict of the eminent commentator Ernst Käsemann contemptuous when he writes: 'Women could not take on legal functions, and according to Revelation, only in heretical circles do prophetesses seem to have had official ecclesiastical powers of leadership.'[245]

It is in any case questionable whether one can speak of legal functions at the time when the early communities were coming into being, since community life was governed by charisma, endowment with the spirit of God. When the community assembled, things were therefore very lively. One person would have a psalm, another teaching to contribute; some had a revelation, others spoke 'in tongues', in other words they presented in an ecstatic discourse what the Spirit of God had directly inspired them to say. However, this did not make sense to all the congregation, so someone was needed to 'translate' the speech. Anyone who could, gave an interpretation. Prophetic discourses had to be judged by the other members of the community (cf. I Cor.14.26ff.). No distinction was made between men and women: anyone who thought that he or she had something to say could speak: 'Any man who prays or speaks prophetically... Any woman who prays or speaks prophetically...' (I Cor.11.4,5). These are the words which Paul uses to describe the community practice that he finds. Such multiplicity causes problems: more than three people speaking with tongues are too many, and in addition they should not all speak together, but one after another, and only one person should interpret them. Anyone who receives a revelation actually in the assembly is to be preferred to the others. For God is not a God of confusion but a God of peace, and all must serve to build up the community (I Cor.14.26ff.). Without questioning charismata, Paul attempts to structure the community assemblies.

So there are focal points. Not everyone has the same gift, not everyone has it in equal measure. The gifts of the spirit enjoy differing respect, and this leads Paul to argue for equality with the picture of the body and its many members: the head cannot say to the feet, 'I do not need you.' What appears lowly is just as important as what seems exalted, for the body cannot do without any of its members; so, too, the community as the body of Christ needs all its members (Rom.12.3-8; I Cor.12.12-31). The Spirit of God is given to all: Jews, Greeks, slaves and free (however, Paul omits men and women in this context; I Cor.12.13).

So it would be inappropriate at this time to speak of offices binding on all communities in terms of church law. *Ekklesia*, church, does not mean the whole church, as it does today, but the particular individual community. Individuals have differing charismata and these give rise to differing functions: an apostle is someone who is called by a direct revelation of the Risen Christ: so this designation is not limited to the 'Twelve' (cf. I Cor.15.3-11). There are deacons, teachers and prophets, also *episcopoi*, probably the leaders of the assembly of presbyters. In addition to that, services to the community are mentioned: miraculous healing, instruction, leading the community, charitable work, 'giving', i.e. the material support of the community. But the form of the community was already changing during the first century. The title presbyter appears only a generation after Paul; the teachers and prophets disappear. It is not possible for us, now, to give a clear outline or a straightforward classification of the functions mentioned. Nor is a distinction made between spiritual activities and organization. Preaching, teaching and functions relating to the leadership of the community merge into one another. And it is impossible to establish a clear relationship between sex and particular tasks. Only at the beginning of the second century is the office of widow mentioned, and that is restricted to charitable works. Cultic designations of office, of a kind that might be expected in connection with the administration of the sacraments, are completely absent.[246]

At the time of the origin and building up of the Christian community the criterion was that of gifts of the Spirit. What happened in the community, which was the testing-ground, demonstrated whether a Christian had such gifts. Therefore the present demand for emancipation in the form of equal rights for men and women cannot be so simply related to that time. 'Women', or their rights or possible disadvantages, are not a theme in the early communities, but not because women were insignificant. This is because it was not a matter of rights. The main theme was the Spirit of God, who calls whom he wills, and a 'right to the Spirit' would go against the nature of this spirit. So there is no 'women's question' either.[247] But that is not to be seen as a retrograde step or a form of life which had not reached the point we have today. The Christians of that time were ahead of our own in that they had fulfilled the requirement which I made at the beginning of this book for transcending feminist theology because they did not have to raise this demand in the first place. And it was that in particular which made the new Christian faith so noteworthy for women in the middle of the first century.

Turning points

Where did these women come from, and why did they come? Some features of life had changed in comparison with the radical exodus existence of the itinerant preachers around Jesus, making Christian discipleship much more tolerable for women and easier to integrate into everyday life.

1. The radical ethos of Jesus, critical of the powers of this world, was an appropriate and practicable answer to those features of life which caused suffering to men and women. But it was also an answer to the pagan critics of the Roman régime; although many had found their place in this empire through profession and status and could live in it, evidently only Jewish faith could give them an ethical orientation – and they became godfearers. The Christian communities then offered complete integration into a binding community where faith in the one God was demonstrated by the way in which the members treated one another as brothers and sisters. The godfearers were mostly recruited from the upper social strata, and in this way independent and active women found an entry into the Christian communities. After the end of the Roman republic there may be said to have been social liberation. Consensus marriage, which was based on a free agreement between the spouses, came to replace the Roman

manus marriage, which subjected the wife to the sole domination of the husband. Marital rights, law, the structure of offices were increasingly reshaped to the advantage of women. We find women in communal politics, in diplomatic service, as property owners or e.g. as tilers; women worked in individual trades as tailors, hairdressers or private secretaries. All this was 'the result of a long-drawn-out process of liberalization and under the influence of Hellenistic forms of thought and life', and as in the period after the Second World War 'on the basis of economic prosperity'.[248] And as today, so then, there were critics of this development among the men, to whom this seemed to be a lapse from good morals. Thus e.g. the emperor Augustus attempted to restore the old ordering of the household in which the women obediently and demurely devoted themselves to wool-working; indeed he shaped his own family as a model of this.[249] So if the independence of women was not undisputed, indeed precisely because it was not, for a Lydia, Prisca or Phoebe the Christian community could become a homeland which did not require them to give up anything that they were. And conversely, what they were and possessed served to build up the communities.

2. Whereas the Jesus group with its proclamation had limited itself to the children of the house of Israel, the communities opened themselves up to Gentiles. As a result not only did emancipated women come to them, but also well-to-do women and men. The radical ethos of the Jesus tradition included renunciation of possessions. In the communities the original ideal of poverty turned into a just distribution of goods: the Christians shared. Whether it happened in the ideal fashion depicted by Luke in Acts (4.32) must be left open. It is certain that 'giving' was regarded as a charisma, and those Christians with property gave for many purposes: the communities met in their houses, they offered hospitality to travellers, they provided complete subsistence for some of the missionaries, they paid for journeys which extended far beyond Palestine, and they also gave money to other communities, not just to their own. At first the poor were also regarded as equal members of the communities, and this preserved their inclusiveness. This relaxation of the radical demand for poverty made it possible for far more people to join the Christian community. Well-to-do women were asked, and when Phoebe is

said to have helped Paul (Rom.16.2), we may suppose that she provided financial support for his journeys.

3. The radical ethos of the Jesus group included renunciation of a fixed abode, but the community settled in one place. The cradle of the local community was the house community. Christian women did not have to leave their home for the sake of the gospel; on the contrary they made it the centre of Christian praxis – certainly a decisive reason for active collaboration. The way in which a person was converted had also changed since the time of Jesus. Instead of the call 'Repent, leave everything and follow me!', not only was the individual baptized, but also the whole house. Lydia, whom I mentioned earlier, was baptized along with her whole house (Acts 16.15), as was the centurion Cornelius in Caesarea (Acts 10.2), the gaoler in Philippi (Acts 16.33), Crispus the president of the synagogue in Corinth (Acts 18.8) or Stephanas (I Cor.1.16; 16.15). The household included the spouse, children and servants. Through such baptismal practice it was no longer just those who had been converted by personal decision who joined the community. The familiar problem of child baptism arose, and the community increasingly turned into a mixed group with all the difficulties that go with that: did they all, could they all know what Christian faith was about?

4. The Christians in the community did not have to give up house, occupation, possessions and family – and this was a decisive change from the hostility to the family in the Jesus tradition. Families were no longer torn apart over belief. Even where the whole family was not baptized at the same time, but baptism was given to just one member of the family, the family nevertheless remained basically intact. There were mixed marriages between Christians and Gentiles, and as long as the pagan partner did not seek separation, he was incorporated in the community and thus 'sanctified' (I Cor.7.12ff.). The same went for Gentile children. Behind this, of course, was the hope that the Gentile partner would also be baptized. This social structure particularly suited women who were tied to home and children and without doubt encouraged their entry into the Christian community. So it is not surprising that the model of the mixed marriage predominates, in which the wife is a Christian and the husband is a pagan.[250] However, in the later period of persecution,

cases increased in which Christian wives had to keep their faith secret from their pagan husbands, in order not to be denounced.[251]

5. The first Christian communities are in a transitional period: some of the followers of Jesus were still alive, and they continued the practice of the itinerant preachers who renounced possessions. However, their life-style was made easier for them by the local communities, since now the communities provided for their support, and not just generous people who heard them preach. Since as former Galilean farmers and fishermen they had forfeited their source of income, they and their families (including their wives) were dependent on this. Alongside them, however, a new type of missionary came into being, which included Paul. These made the foundation of the community their task and partly – like Paul as a craftsman – could earn their own living, so as not to be a burden on the community. On their long journeys through the Eastern Mediterranean they found incomparably more support in the communities than was the case for the radical Jesus group, which had no communities. As such a missionary, man or woman, one did not have to be on the road all the time, but could spend some time in a hospitable community – again a development which favoured the involvement of women with family and children. In addition to the old-style itinerant preachers and the new-style missionaries mention can also be made of travellers who, like Prisca and Aquila, were not pioneers in new missionary territory but devoted themselves to building up the community in already existing Christian areas by founding their own house community. Thus the life of Christians around the middle of the first century took very varied forms and gave people of different origins and status, of both sexes, the possibility of realizing their Christian convictions in terms of their own capacities and possibilities. The contribution of women at all levels of praxis is not to be ignored here.

Paul in contradictions

Paul found all that in existence when he was called by the Risen Christ to be an apostle. He appeared at a time of change and transition which, despite all positive new possibilities, contained within it potent seeds of conflict. So we should not idealize this time either, though Luke does that to a considerable extent, an approach that he has in common with some feminist theologians of our day. Transitions never take place without crises developing, and we only do justice to the person of Paul if we understand him in terms of this history. But what are the main points of the crisis?

While it is true that the dispute between Peter and Paul as to whether Gentiles who were baptized should also observe the Jewish ritual laws, and above all circumcision, was settled at the Apostolic Council in Jerusalem in AD 44/48 in favour of Paul and thus against the observation of the law, the Gentiles who came from another social and cultural context nevertheless introduced their own conceptions, customs and usages into the Christian communities. That inevitably led to tensions, especially as people tend to hang on to that with which they are familiar. Even Paul himself did not avoid such inner conflicts, and these had external consequences.

Paul was a Jew; he had had a rabbinic training, and before the Risen Christ appeared to him he was one of the radicals among his fellow countrymen who fought against the Christian heresy. That he came from Tarsus, a Hellenistic state, and had the privilege of being a Roman citizen, did not prevent him from identifying with the faith of his Jewish forefathers. That is the presupposition for understanding I Cor.11.2-16, which seems clearly to show his hostility to women.

Paul is dealing with a custom which is natural to a Jew. That only becomes clear, however, in v.16, so one has to read the section in the light of the end. The subject under discussion is the custom that Jewish women should wear a veil, at least in worship. The veil was the distinguishing mark of Jewish women in public.[252]

Gentile women did not have this custom. Now as former Jewish women and Gentile women met in the Christian community, the question arose as to which custom was to be favoured. Paul, the former Jew, is familiar with the veil. He says so openly: we do not have this custom, namely of going without a veil (v.16). You cannot blame someone for keeping to customs which have been familiar to him since his childhood. However, the amount of argumentation with which Paul defends this custom and wants to make it a rule in the community is amazing.

He begins with a clear hierarchy: 'I want you to understand

that the head of every man is Christ, the head of a woman is her husband, and the head of Christ is God' (v.3). Then he goes over to the situation in worship: 'Any man who prays or prophesies with his head covered dishonours his head' (v.4). There now follows a parallel in connection with this appearance, and Paul himself had to acknowlege that there was already a contradiction here to his sexual hierarchy: 'But any woman who prays or prophesies' – now follows the different evaluation - 'with her head unveiled dishonours her head' (v.5).

In the next step Paul again changes levels, away from theological argumentation to a justification of the custom: a woman without a veil is like one with a shorn head, i.e., she can cut her hair off or make herself bald (v.6). Paul then goes back to theology and continues the initial argument: a man should not cover his head 'since he is the image and glory of God' (v.7). He next tries to use the second creation account as a scriptural proof: 'For man was not made from woman, but woman from man' (v.8) – an allusion to the story of the rib, and again: 'Neither was man created for a woman, but woman for man' (v.9) – an allusion to the woman as man's helpmeet. Then follows a mythological statement: 'That is why a woman ought to have a veil on her head, because of the angels' (v.10). Here Paul is probably thinking of the wicked angels in Gen.6.1f., who ensnare human women. The veil is therefore to be understood as protection against the demons; the woman needs this special protection as she is not in the image of God. Here Paul has long since left the level of custom and he argues, in a way which we still find familiar, from the divine ordering of creation – and does so in terms of a rabbinic exegesis of the text of the Old Testament which in the first creation story attributes being in the image of God to human beings as man and women (Gen.1.27).

Now it suddenly strikes Paul where his interest in a custom has taken him – right into the middle of his former rabbinical existence. He corrects himself and breaks off: 'But,' the Christian Paul now says, 'in the Lord woman is not independent of man nor man of woman; for as woman was made from man, so man is now born of woman' (vv.11,12). Rabbinic exegesis does not work 'in the Lord', and so Paul denies all previous theological statements which were meant to justify wearing a veil.

Then Paul returns to the level which is more appropriate for the theme, namely that of custom: 'Judge for yourselves; is it proper for a woman to pray to God with her head uncovered?' he asks the community (v.13). As the apostle did not succeed in providing a justification in terms of the theology of creation, he now tries a kind of justification in terms of natural law: nature itself teaches that for men long hair is a shame while for women it is an honour (vv.14,15). Here there is no further need of exegesis of the text, since the contemporary reader is immediately and directly involved in the debate whether one should allow young men and schoolboys their long hair or whether grown men with long hair can still be 'real' men.

And Paul gallops off once again, this time without noticing that he has got himself entangled in a contradiction: as long hair is an honour, and long hair to some degree veils a woman, he now uses long hair as an argument for the veil. But this is not conclusive, because Gentile women, too, have long hair. So again he has found no convincing argument for the veil. Thus he ends his discussion with the lapidary statement: 'We have no such custom as going without a veil.' He could have limited himself to this statement.

As the textual tradition is unanimous, the wealth of contradictions cannot go back to contradictions in the tradition. Were these contradictions between the community and Paul, so that Paul was reproducing a community view with his rabbinic exegesis? That, too, must be ruled out, since the apostle begins decisively: 'I want you to know that...' So the contradictions cannot lie only with Paul himself. The expenditure of argument and indeed emotion suggests that Paul himself has a problem: within him there is a conflict between theory and praxis, between the knowledge that in Christ men have no advantage over women or *vice versa* (cf.vv.11,12), and the inner emotional link with a familiar practice – women wear veils. In the light of this contradiction he is not free enough to accept women without veils. Here he might not have found things so difficult had he argued for uncircumcised men. Paul knows the gospel that he preaches to Jews and Gentiles all over the world, but sometimes he has difficulty in acting in accordance with it – a familiar phenomenon to us.

Why should an apostle be completely free from such contradictions? Even those who are called as charismatics remain human beings. How often were the disciples of Jesus reproached for their lack of faith! Anyone who does not to take account of such weaknesses and regards Paul as an undisputed authority in every sentences will not do justice to him where he has something to say. Paul would object if one did not take his own correction seriously and pinned him to what he himself had begun to find doubtful. As in an argument between two living people, so too in one with someone who is dead, it is unfair to fix on an argument which the other party contradicts. But that happens when Paul is accused of justifiying the inferiority of women with a theology of creation. Depending on which verse one chooses one can find in this short section alone both arguments for the claim of the gospel and the abolition of the difference between the sexes and arguments against. The Pauline texts lend themselves very easily to exploitation for one's own interest; that is why the history of their exegesis has also been so ambiguous and contradictory. However, it would be a great step forward if Paul helped his readers to self-knowledge, to recognition of the contradiction between theory and practice in one's own thought and action. At any rate Paul could correct himself, whereas most of his successors were incapable of doing so.

An ascetic remains realistic

Both the Christians of the earliest period and Paul were and are continually accused of having failed to implement the claim of the gospel, since social structures remained untouched by it. There are no programmatic texts on the liberation of women; on the contrary all, including slaves, are called on to remain in the state in which they are (I Cor 7.20-24). So what has Christian faith, the critics ask, contributed to the world? As so often, in such questions the criteria of present experience and present interest are introduced into a reality which must be distinguished from them. First, Paul and the Christians of his time did not have the intention of 'improving' the world by changing its structures, i.e. independently of the faith and life of the community. The Pauline plea for remaining in the state one is, holds before God (v.24) and thus in the community of Christians, for whom the question of status thus becomes irrelevant. Secondly, this attitude does not mean refusal to engage in any alteration of socially relevant action. Only, the practice of Christians is 'subversive'; it undermines the ordinances which normally apply in the world. When Paul says that everyone is to remain in his or her present status, his view is that the status is insignificant for Christians.[253] However, that presupposes a common and binding conviction and attitude among Christians. Where there is no such presupposition, the usual customs and immoralities appear, and at that point a change of status offers misleading privileges for those on the upper levels. Renunciation, giving, service are Christian charismata which not everyone has, or which not everyone has to the same extent. The heart is often more attached to what is important in the world which Christians have left behind.

The increasing number of Christians and communities, contact between different ethnic groups, a baptismal practice which no longer presupposes a change of heart in the strict sense, all that leads to no longer taking the claim of Gal.3.28 quite so seriously. Then apparent incidentals like a familiar habit can become the most important thing. So too among the Christians of the first century the ordinances of the world once more slowly gain the upper hand over against the ordinance of God. Thus Christian faith brought something decisively new to the world, but not everyone understood that and realized it in their actions.

The conflict between former Jews and former Gentiles in the Christian communities turned out entirely in favour of the Gentiles, simply because those who had remained Jews fought against the Christian heresy and destroyed the hopes of Christians that all Jews would be converted. Disillusioned, even the Jew Paul can find evil words about his contemporaries. You have, he writes to the Gentile-Christian community in Thessalonica, had to suffer persecution from your own people, as the Jewish-Christian communities in Judaea have had to suffer it from theirs, 'who killed the Lord Jesus; and they persecuted the prophets and now us' (I Thess.2.14-16). Finally Paul calls down the wrath of God upon the Jews. Here, too, he speaks emotionally and says things which he does not repeat in Romans (9-11), which he wrote later. Is he therefore antisemitic? Certainly not. But what was said about I Cor.11.2-16 also applies here: a similar selection of texts can be used to indicate an antisemitic concern. But this procedure tells against Paul's interpreters rather than against Paul himself.

That there is no hierarchy betwen the sexes in the Christian community is, to begin with, a very abstract claim. How can this be realized in 'normal' circumstances which are not shaped by the exodus? The Corinthians were faced with this question and Paul attempted to answer it (I Cor.7). His first sentence seems to confirm all the evil accusations which women make against Paul out of hostility towards him: 'It is well for a man not to touch a woman.' This statement, however, is in a context which must be examined more closely. Verse 1 can be translated in two ways: 'Concerning what you have written, namely that it is well for a man not to touch a woman...', or 'Concerning what you have written (I say to you) it is well for a man not to touch a woman.' In one case Paul would be quoting an opinion or a question from the Corinthians, and in the other he would be expressing his opinion on a question not asked explicitly by the Corinthians. Which of the two variants is more probable emerges from the subsequent course of the text: 'But because of immorality, each man should give to his wife her conjugal rights, and likewise the wife to her husband. For the wife does not rule over her own body, but the husband does; likewise the husband does not rule over his own body, but the wife does' (vv.2-4). There is more to be said in favour of the first variant: Paul is asked by the Corinthians whether as a Christian one must live ascetically in sexual matters. His answer is 'No'. Initially it is striking that Paul speaks of wife and husband on completely equal terms. There is no mention of the subjection of the wife. Each needs the other and therefore each is indebted to the other. The couple are not to abstain from each other too long and everything is to be done in harmony (the Greek word for this is *symphonia*). Nor does Paul begin from the widespread prejudice that men are more susceptible to sexual temptations than women. Both can be led astray. Paul shows himself to be a realist: where men and women live together in a community, in a house, and do not go through the country without possessions, without a home, practising sexual asceticism, a new problem arises. Paul's solution is that marriage preserves one from a libertinism which destroys the community.

Is this to be taken as a statement which is hostile to women or to the body? Feminists today rightly denounce the libertinism of 'sexual liberation' as being a burden to women, if in addition they are still tied to children. Any form of liberalization leads to an accentuation of the social imbalance, in that it again benefits those who are already privileged: those who are free become even freer and those who are not, are robbed of their last bit of freedom, as one might say with an alteration to Luke 19.26.

When Paul speaks of sexual freedom, immorality or fornication (Greek *porneia*), he is also thinking of intercourse with prostitutes. He deals with this problem in I Cor.6.12-20, from which it emerges that the Corinthians were not unaffected by it. His first argument is that sexuality is not a merely natural function, like eating and drinking, since it binds two people together. Nor is the body merely body or of less value than spirit or soul, but it is the visible place for the proving of faith. Just as all faith is 'embodied' by giving corresponding form to this faith in a community, so too is the Christian faith, if it is realized authentically. The criterion which governs union with a prostitute, heightened pleasure, has nothing to do with what is important among Christians. Therefore someone who goes to a prostitute sins against his own body (v.18): he violates and abandons Christian fellowship and through the prostitute is incorporated into a world in which people are concerned for pleasure and other gain, and dominate one another.[254] That is not how things are to be among Christians, for the body is a temple of the spirit of God (v.19).

Not only do preaching and words communicate something of what is valid among human beings; reality itself speaks. Therefore, conversely, Gentiles can be incorporated into the Christian community so far as they want to be. The unbelieving husband is 'sanctified' by the Christian wife, says Paul, and *vice versa*: the same goes for their children (I Cor.7.10-16). Here the apostle is replying to a further problem in the Corinthian community which has allowed entry to Gentiles: mixed marriages. Jesus' prohibition against divorce which Paul quotes to begin with (vv.10-11) was not made in connection with mixed marriages. Therefore Paul looks for an interpretation which is appropriate to the situation and in accord with the spirit of Jesus, which he also declares to be his own view – he does not legitimate it through a saying of the Lord. The Christian partner is bound to the marriage, but the Gentile partner can go if he or she does not like it among the Christians. Free will is the supreme command, and even the

Christian partner must not compel himself or herself and the
partner who believes otherwise to remain in a marriage while the
other protests against it. Peace is more important than the
commandment (v.15). And as there is no guarantee that the
Christian half can convert the non-Christian half, this must be
left to God (vv.16-17). Paul is looking for a solution without any
pressure on the conscience. Could not the present-day church
appeal to this to its own advantage?

Should Christians live as sexual ascetics? No, says Paul, but he
adds a qualification: the no is a concession, not an order (v.6). He
personally would like it best if all people lived an unmarried life
as he does (v.7). So those who are married should not separate,
but those who are single or widowed should not seek marriage.
Here Paul is not preaching the gospel but expressing a wish for
which he can also give a reason: the married have 'worldly
troubles' and Paul would gladly see them spared those (v.28). He
does not go into more detail about what he is thinking, but it is
fairly clear what he means: birth, the mortality of mothers and
children, the daily concern of keeping them alive and seeing to
the upbringing of the children. Tertullian already understood Paul
correctly.[255] Moreover married people seek to please each other
and thus fall short in concern for the things of the Lord (vv.32-
34). Here Paul does not deprecate pleasure as an erotic component
in the relationship but regards it as being necessary.[256] But anyone
who wants to devote his or her life to the service of the gospel is
better off living singly, like Paul. Paul speaks in favour of –
voluntary – celibacy and in so doing could again be taken as a
model by his later followers. It is striking that Paul had hardly
any effect on subsequent history in what he said here on the
question of mixed marriages, but the rabbinic 'howler' of I Cor.11
is on everyone's lips.

Is Paul really so hostile to the body and to women when he
warns against the consequences of marriage and bringing up
children? At all events he warns both partners, including the
husband, whereas today only women are faced with the alternative
of either devoting themselves to a job or marrying and bringing
up children. For men, again, is a matter of 'to him who has it will
be given', since the husband needs the wife as a support and to
free him from burdens, if he is really to devote himself to a career.

The Protestant manse exploited this for several centuries, arguing that the pastor's wife and even his children were in the service of the 'spiritual' pastor. The present crisis over this model often leads to divorce.

But where a woman decides against husband, children and family and for a job, without a husband, even down to modern times, she is regarded as only 'half a person', if not as a compulsive neurotic. By contrast, Paul's view is that life without marriage can be seen as a form of life which is significant and fulfilled in itself. Here Paul is not saying that sexuality and marriage are sin, as he is so often supposed to. He explicitly rejects this view (v.28).

As an apostle and charismatic Paul has opted for celibacy, and that he can do so he owes to the grace of God. Not everyone can (v.7), for grace is not at our disposal. Here Paul sees, realistically, that liberation from pleasure is also liberation from a burden. In this attitude he is a disciple of Jesus and his radical ethos. He does not struggle laboriously for his renunciation against the compulsions of the 'flesh', but practises it for the sake of the gospel, which is more important to him than anything else. Women who adopt his course do not therefore forfeit their fulfilment by not having a husband. In the Christian community, as a pledge of the new creation, neither marriage not lack of marriage are among the sixty-four thousand dollar questions.

Paul has already often proved to be a realist, and therefore he is well aware why most people do not follow his example. Unfulfilled erotic desire often eats away at the hearts and actions of human beings. Before that happens, before sexual needs possibly lead to unbridled lust, it is necessary to get married (vv.5,9,36f.). In his letters Paul constantly goes into problems which are typical of the transition from the exodus model to the community model. He practises the exodus model with some qualifications, but it cannot be lived out by a house community. He recognizes both forms of life: it is good to marry, but it is equally good, if not better, to remain unmarried (v.38).[257] Paul thinks that marriage is good as a remedy for incontinence: marry before you are consumed by desire! However, this understanding of marriage to which e.g. the Reformers appeal as justification for the marriage of priests runs the risk of demoting the partner to being a kind of lightning conductor for one's own desires. But this theme can be assessed in both a negative and a positive way. It can be assessed in a negative way, in that marriage is regarded simply as a concession to those who are poor and weak and cannot master their 'urges'; or positively, in that this model deals realistically with the power of sexuality and therefore does not seek to compel asceticism at any price. Paul sees both sides. That as an apostle he goes by the practice of the Jesus group is his decision, but he does not make it into a law for everyone. Anyone who refers to Paul for an understanding of marriage must, however, reflect that here is a man who is seeking to live out radical discipleship in the style of Jesus and who has received his own celibacy as a charisma, as a gift of the grace of God. There is no evidence of hostility to the body or to women in Paul, and one can accept the fact that as a voluntary ascetic his understanding is not great where love is concerned. I sometimes wish that those who champion a sexual libertinism had as much understanding for ascetics as the ascetic Paul has for eroticism and sexuality.

The charge that Paul has turned the 'good' Jesus tradition into a bad one makes one individual illegitimately responsible for social change in the communities. The individualization of problems of social structure is a popular but inadequate attempt to master the conflicts by exclusively referring them to the sphere of ethical decision.[258] However, though Paul himself practises the life-style of the immediate followers of Jesus, he attempts to solve the new questions which arise in the spirit of Jesus Christ. How can Gentiles be integrated into the community? What is the significance of the renunciation of possessions, home and marriage for the Christian self-understanding and the structures ordering Christian communities? How can unity among communities be brought about when they are increasing in number and geographical spread? How does one deal with the increasing number of heretical groups inside and outside the communities? The most attractive and most challenging heresy of antiquity was Gnosticism. Where did it come from, why did it arise and what did it mean for the history of Christian women?

CHAPTER SIX

Emanations and Syzygies: Gnosticism

When Elaine Pagels brought out her book *The Gnostic Gospels* in 1979, there was a stir in feminist circles: in a chapter entitled 'God the Father/God the Mother' she presented a feminist reading of Gnostic texts, and she gave significance to this enterprise by regarding Gnosticism in principle as a Christian heresy which supplemented, and indeed corrected, false developments in orthodoxy. How firm is the foundation on which these assumptions are based?

It is striking, says Pagels, that Gnostic texts 'continually use sexual symbolism to describe God'.[259] These would hardly be pagan elements from the goddess tradition, as the language of these texts is 'specifically Christian, unmistakably related to a Jewish heritage'.[260] God, who in Gnosticism is regarded as the ineffable one, brings forth all the 'emanations' of the divine being from herself, 'ranged in harmonious pairs of masculine and feminine energies'.[261] Granted, Pagels points out that such sexual concepts are not to be understood literally but symbolically; nevertheless she derives them from the fact that there was 'a correlation between religious theory and social practice'.[262] It can be regarded as proven that women in the Gnostic communities had considerably more prominent functions and positions than in the orthodox communities. Pagels sees the foundation for this in the superiority of the feminine Sophia, which stands at the centre of many Gnostic myths.[263] Finally, she puts forward the theory that the pre-eminent role of women in Gnostic communities is the reason why the orthodox Christians condemned Gnosticism as a heresy and fought against it – with ultimate success.[264] The Gnostic texts should challenge us, Pagels says in formulating her interest, 'to reinterpret history – and to re-evaluate the present situation'.[265]

Not only its assessment of women and the – apparent – lack of conflict between the sexes makes Gnosticism seem to Pagels the 'more reasonable' variant of Christianity. 'Gnostic Christians undoubtedly expressed ideas that the orthodox abhorred. For example, some of these gnostic texts question whether all suffering, labour, and death derive from human sin, which, in the orthodox version, marred an originally perfect creation. Others speak of the feminine element in the divine, celebrating God as Father *and* Mother. Still others suggest that Christ's resurrection is to be understood symbolically, not literally.'[266] Pagels contrasts this with the views of orthodox Christianity, which she thinks would now be more alien to us than those of Gnosticism. 'The creed requires, for example, that Christians confess that God is perfectly good, and still, he created a world that includes pain, injustice and death; that Jesus of Nazareth was born of a virgin mother; and that after being executed by order of the Roman procurator, Pontius Pilate, he arose from the grave "on the third day".'[267]

Pagels' picture of orthodoxy is no more sophisticated than that of Gnosticism. But despite the manifest contradictions which she sees beween the two in the sphere of religious conceptions, she assumes that the battle against Gnosticism was a battle against its social implications and therefore not least against the position of women in the Gnostic communities. Here Pagels wants to put aside the question of the origin of Gnosticism,[268] to which there is hardly an answer, and limit herself to those sources which can be characterized as Christian Gnosticism. Her aim is to see what can be derived from such texts about the origin of Christianity.[269] That is indeed the question, and it is illuminating to make a critical examination of Elaine Pagels' answer to it by means of the texts of Gnosticism and the New Testament.[270]

In search of the 'better' Christian

Gnosticism is a term used to summarize a religious attitude and practice which seems to derive the motives for its views from many different religions and world-views and in so doing nevertheless demonstrates a new and independent position.

Gnosticism can appear pagan, Jewish and Christian.[271] Chronologically, its origin roughly coincides with the origin of Christianity; geographically Gnosticism extends throughout the Mediterranean area. In Manichaeism[272] Gnosticism reached as far as the Eastern provinces of Iran and to Chinese Turkestan, where in the eighth century it was elevated to the role of a state religion.[273] The Christian Gnostics were regarded as a danger by the early church not least because they understood themselves to possess the true Christian teaching and put forward reinterpretations of the Christian creed with great conviction. In Mandaeism, a sect with Jewish and Christian elements which presumably also came into being in the time of Jesus, Gnosticism has even survived to the present day. The baptismal sect of the Mandaeans is to be found in southern Iraq and in south-western Iran and numbers about 5000 members.[274]

The heyday of Gnosticism falls in the second century. In a later period the vigorous fight against it by the church also led to hardening within Gnosticism, to the 'dogmatizing' of the Gnostic mythologies and to the repudiation of controversies. That is not surprising, since the persecution of the Gnostics went as far as physical extermination. From the fourth century on, state and church systematically destroyed the Gnostic literature: Gnosticism was able to survive about 500 years before it finally succumbed to its more powerful opponent, the church.

Until a few decades ago Gnosticism was accessible to us almost exclusively through the descriptions and quotations in those writings of the church fathers which sought to refute Gnosticism. The church fathers probably had Gnostic writings in front of them, but it must remain open whether they always quoted them correctly; it is even more questionable whether we can get at the way in which the Gnostics understood themselves where their statements are only quoted by way of references. I have already demonstrated that understanding is fraught with problems;[275] at all events the church fathers were interested in deprecating Gnosticism as a heresy, though most of them are amazingly accurate in their description of it.

Today research into Gnosticism is no longer carried on from a heresiological perspective; new discoveries of original Gnostic texts have given decisive stimulus to it. In 1945 an Arab farmer in the neighbourhood of present-day Nag Hammadi (the old Chenoboskion) in Upper Egypt by chance discovered jars which contained a total of 13 codexes (51 works and 1130 pages) in Coptic.[276] The texts had evidently been hidden there. Certainly individual missionaries and travellers had previously discovered Gnostic texts in eastern markets,[277] but the wealth of the Nag Hammadi finds took scholarship a good deal further. The texts have meanwhile been edited and translated into many languages.[278]

The way in which Elaine Pagels quotes the sources gives the uninitiated reader the impression that there was a well-thought out overall context for Gnostic sayings.[279] But this impression is misleading and can arise only because the various writings are not differentiated in time, order or character, and original texts and quotations from the church fathers stand side by side. Moreover Pagels does not take into account the fact that some of the texts (e.g. the Gospels of Thomas and Philip, the Book of Thomas the Contender and the Valentinian evidence) have a clear Christian character whereas others are only loosely connected with Christianity (e.g. the Paraphrase of Shem or the Apocryphon of John with its detailed mythology).

Now what is new and special about Gnosticism that makes it a distinctive religious trend? The self-understanding of a Gnostic can be most appropriately expressed by the statement 'Remember that you are a god'. All the Gnostic anthropology hangs on that: man has a spirit-self which is thought to be substantially divine. This divine nucleus of being, metaphorically described as light or a spark of light, is trapped in matter, i.e. in the body, by the powers of darkness; in addition these powers have made man lapse into anaesthesia, into unconsciousness, so that he knows nothing of his divine spirit-self. Therefore he needs gnosis, know-ledge, to remind himself of his divine origin, a knowledge which already has redemptive effect because it breaks the power of darkness and is the presupposition for escaping the jaws of darkness. Hence, 'Remember that you are a God'.

According to the Gnostic conception man is tripartite. He consists of the divine spirit-self, in the texts called spirit, reason or even soul; the body, matter, which holds the spirit-self captive; and the soul, which presents itself to the Gnostic as a personal demonic power. Often the third element disappears in favour of a bipartite division into the two conflicting powers of the divine spirit-self and corporeal matter. This dualism is typical of gnosticism. Now if a man shares in the knowledge of the way in which he is made he is one of the pneumatics, whereas people without such knowledge are hylics (from the Greek *hyle*, matter); in other words they are trapped in matter without knowing it. As they do not live in awareness of their divine origin they remain in the hands of the powers of darkness, cannot be redeemed, and perish: they are dead and remain dead. Between them are the psychics: although they have no gnosis, they can participate in salvation if they follow the ethical precepts (in Christian Gnosticism these are the precepts of the mainstream church), though these remain external to them. In other words they have to submit themselves to a legal framework which the pneumatic does not need because of his deeper insight.[280] So the Gnostic understands himself as a god or part of the divine caught in anti-godly matter.

It is striking that already in an early form of Gnostic systematization,[281] in the texts of Simonian Gnosticism, themes are dominant which from the perspective of a feminist interest cannot be regarded as desirable, like the suspicious role which a 'fallen' feminine being plays in Gnostic conceptions (we shall have to consider this again later). Simon is the only Gnostic to appear in the New Testament. According to Acts 8.9ff. he amazes the people of Samaria through witchcraft and attracts large numbers of followers. Already here and even more clearly through the testimony of the church fathers Justin and Irenaeus of Lyons, who take issue with Simonian Gnosticism,[282] it becomes clear that Simon has himself worshipped by his fellow countrymen as a god.[283]

The same is true of his companion, 'a woman named Helena, who travelled around with him on those days and had formerly been a public prostitute'; she is called 'the first Ennoia (= thought) begotten by him'.[284] She is said to be 'the mother of all, by whom, in the beginning, he conceived in his mind the plan of forming angels and archangels'.[285] But these powers and angels have Helena in their grasp so that she cannot return to the Father, to the supreme God. Their motive is envy. They do not want to be regarded as descendants of the supreme God but as unbegotten gods, independent demons. Therefore they imprison Ennoia in a human body, a feminine body, to add to her shame.

So finally she ends up in a brothel in Tyre. The supreme God himself must now come in the form of Simon to free his Ennoia: 'he had descended, transfigured and assimilated to powers and principalities and angels, so that he might appear among men to be a man, while yet he was not a man.'[286] In this way not only is Ennoia freed, but any man who languishes in the prison of matter, when he joins Simon.[287]

Valentinus,[288] the most brilliant Christian Gnostic of the second century, whose school proved itself to be the most able adversary in the battle with the opponents of Gnosticism, makes the destiny of a feminine divine figure, Sophia, responsible for human destiny: through the fall of this feminine light-being the light as the spirit-self of mankind falls into the captivity of lower matter. Like the light-being, so too mankind needs redemption which is brought about by a male divine figure.[289]

This basic conception of Gnostic anthropology, the dualism of the divine spirit-self of man and matter hostile to God – intrinsically not a very Christian conception[290] – does not come out clearly enough in Elaine Pagels' description and argument. The fault lies in the method: Pagels works in terms of the history of motives. That begins with the way in which she refers to those Gnostic texts which display motives from Jewish-Christian religious circles. She then argues from the Christian themes to a Chistian origin: 'Much of the literature discovered at Nag Hammadi is distinctively Christian.'[291] And she goes on to conclude that Gnosticism offers 'alternative forms of early Christianity'.[292] In Pagels' view the repudiation of Gnosticism by orthodox Christians is grounded in the greater power of conviction in the Gnostic variants, since as a 'philosophy of pessimism'[293] Gnosticism had more plausible answers to the social and political crisis of the first century for alienated men in need of redemption.[294] So according to Pagels the Gnostics are the 'better' Christians.

The motive-historical method proceeds by taking particular themes which it regards as essential and characteristic and then comparing them with themes in other texts in order to produce causal connections. According to the Vienna Coptologist Robert Haardt the concept of the motive, which here has nothing to do with the motives of human action, denotes 'the objectifications of the level of testimony which can be identified by literary criticism...' Causal connections are postulated between these successive historical objectifications without there necessarily always having to be (or being able to be) insight into the real circumstances in which the objectifications of the level of testimony came into existence; sometimes such causal connections are presupposed as being evident.'[295]

That is what Pagels practises; she presupposes as being evident what is not evident. One has to know the limits of the motive-historical method in order to be able to understand why in the history of research into Gnosticism people have come to very different conclusions. For in the attempt to derive Gnosticism from other religious systems, the texts can also be selected in terms of other motives, those which then argue for an Iranian, Platonic, Jewish or other origin for Gnosticism.[296] To follow Robert Haardt again: 'The reconstruction of historical phenomena and facts is not independent of the particular horizon of motivation of the time in which they are set and of the researcher who brings the fact to appearance in its particular facticity... Thus the nature, the history, and the history of the interpretation of Gnosticism are communicated through one another.'[297] While, therefore, many motives in the Gnostic texts are Christian, decidedly non-Christian motives can also be found. So we cannot simply begin from the fact that the Gnostics were 'alternative' Christians. If Pagels does that she may be formulating her heuristic interest but she is far from offering 'assured' results of research.

A second trend of motive-historical research in Pagels begins from a feminist interest. Again she divides the texts into their constituent motives, taking them out of their original context in order to make them into a new construction in the context of present feminist questions and wishes. But here too that dialectic should be remembered, which, if it shatters into irreconcilable oppositions, furthers error and no longer serves any interest: a motive receives its significance from the context in which it occurs and the overall context is formed by the motives. Individual elements are mostly not new but a new context can give them a new significance. Again the self-understanding of the people who arrange the motives is responsible for that self-understanding. So while Gnosticism has its dualistic anthropology in common with Platonism, Platonism and Gnosticism are not identical. The individual motives must be combined into a kind of 'basic structure',[298] but that then again shows a high degree of abstraction and is again made specific through the motives, but not put together summarily. Only in a complex process of this kind is it possible to grasp something of the 'essence' of a religious tradition, in which the heuristic interest of a scholar must always be taken into account, so that one perceives it as such and does not secretly – like Pagels – present it as a fact.

An androgynous god?

Elaine Pagels writes that the god of the Gnostics is to be considered masculo-feminine, i.e. androgynous, and is called Metropator ('Mother-Father').[299] Let us test that by the texts themselves. Gnosticism developed a series of myths which are extensive and to our sensibilities abstruse,[300] through which it 'explains' the tension of human existence between divine spirit-self and matter. Gnostic texts are very difficult to understand because they provide a bewildering multiplicity of forms, concepts and conceptions. As these texts belong to different cultural and religious groups and come from different centuries, and there are often also inconsistencies within one and the same work, a systematic account is difficult. That should be said first before we look at the wording of the sources.

I begin with the Apocryphon of John, a very popular second-century writing (before 180) which has undergone a Christian revision and has been handed down in four versions.[301] It offers an extensive mythology and Pagels also uses it as evidence for her theory of an androgynous Gnostic image of God. John, one of the sons of Zebedee, receives a special revelation from Jesus. A boy appears to him in a vision in the form of an old man, bathed in light, and says: 'I am the one who is with you for ever. I am the Father, I am the Mother, I am the Son.'[302] Pagels sees this as a description of God, although the overall context clearly shows that here Jesus is speaking of himself. Her comment is therefore at the least highly inaccurate.

Only in the further course of the text does there follow teaching by John through the revealer about the supreme God, with whom no androgynous conceptions are associated:

The Monad is a monarchy with nothing above it. It is he who exists as God and Father of everything, the invisible one who is above everything, who is imperishability; existing as pure light which no eye can behold. He is the invisible Spirit; it is not right to think about him as a god or something similar. For he is more than a god, since there is no one above him... He has no need of anything for he is completely perfect... He is illimitable because there is no one prior to him to limit him. He is unsearchable because there exists no one prior to him to examine him. He is immeasurable because there was no one prior to him to measure him. He is invisible because no one saw him... He is ineffable because no one could comprehend him to speak about him. He is unnameable because there is no one prior to him to name him... He is not in perfection nor in blessedness nor in divinity, but being far superior. He is not corporeal nor incorporeal. He is not great and not small. It is not possible to say 'What is his quantity' or 'What is his quality', for no one can know him... his essence does not belong to the aeons nor to time... His aeon is indestructible, at rest and being in silence, reposing.[303]

This text shows that the Gnostics love 'negative theology' – they speak of God through the *via negationis*: they say what God is not at all, and that it is impossible to imagine him; indeed even the statement that he is divine is already too specific for what is unimaginable.[304] Pagels accuses Christian theologians of being too quick to point out 'that God is not to be considered in sexual terms at all. Yet the actual language they use daily in worship and prayer conveys a different message', namely that God is male.[305] Apt though this criticism is, the Gnostics are hardly suitable as an alternative. The Apocryphon of John and other Gnostic writings speak repeatedly of the supreme God as the Father, and where they avoid doing so, they in no way lapse into an androgynous way of speaking. They do precisely that of which Pagels accuses Christian theologians: they dispense with all positive human categories, including sexual ones. This is matched by a form of prayer characteristic of Gnosticism: 'Hear me as I praise you, mystery that exists before all that is incomprehensible and infinite.

Hear me as I praise you, mystery that emanates into its mystery, so that the mystery existing from the beginning is fulfilled.'[306]

However, the conception of male-female harmony which can be found throughout Gnostic texts does certainly refer to the emanations of the unimaginable God. The Apocryphon of John again shows us what that means: the Unimaginable now sees his image in pure light-water.[307]

> And his Ennoia performed a deed and she came forth, namely she who had appeared before him in the shine of his light. This is the first power which was before all of them and which came forth from his mind, that is the Pronoia (= providence) of the All. Her light... is the image of the invisible, virginal Spirit who is perfect. The first power, the glory, Barbelo, the perfect glory... she praised him because thanks to him she had come forth. This (= the virgin spirit) is the first thought, his image; she became the womb of everything for she is prior to them all, the thrice-male, the thrice-powerful, the thrice-named androgynous one.[308]

A variant of the text reads:

> This is the first Ennoia, his image. She became a first man; he is the virgin spirit, the thrice-male, the one with three hymns, three names, three power, the aeon, who does not grow old, an androgyne who emerged from her Pronoia.[309]

A characteristic feature of the Gnostic myth is the emanations, divine essences which the Unimaginable, the pure light, sends out from himself and which are ordered in male-female pairs (syzygies). These emanations take place in a kind of chain reaction. Ennoia produces Prognosis (= prior knowledge), Prognosis Aphtharsia (= incorruptibility), Aphtharsia Eternal Life, and so on in numerous bifurcations down to the male-female Dekas (tenness).

The sections which I have quoted already indicate a more diverse picture than that given by Elaine Pagels. The Gnostic God, the Unimaginable, an abundance of pure light, is only defined more closely by the emanations which are distinct from him. As we shall see in due course, he is in no way identical with the Christian God. He emanates a wealth of entities which are, however, understood in very abstract terms: thought, foreknowledge, incorruptibility and so on. These entities fill the light world, but in hierarchy are clearly below the pure light. They are the first to be defined in male-female terms, so that it is misleading to say that Gnostic conceptions of God were androgynous. In addition, the Gnostic heaven cannot directly be compared with the heaven of the Bible: Pagels is not comparing like with like.

So it is the emanations which are in fact thought of in male-female terms. They live in syzygies: each light being has its consort of the opposite sex. However, these pairs are characterized precisely by the fact that they are not bound together in sexual desire. In the myth of the original harmonious unity of the syzygies the polar tension of the sexes is done away with. So the tension which is given along with sexuality is accordingly denied the perfection which prevails in the world of light. In the section of text from the *Apophasis Megale*[310] quoted by Pagels the abolition of the polarity comes out particularly clearly: from the power of silence there appears (as an emanation) the great power, 'divided above and below; generating itself, making itself grow, seeking itself, finding itself, being mother of itself, father of itself, sister of itself, spouse of itself, daughter of itself, son of itself – mother, father, unity, being a source of the entire circle of existence'.[311] The abolition of the tension between the sexes in myth is matched – as we shall see in due course – by the practice of sexual asceticism.

The abolition of the difference between the sexes as the intention of male-female conceptions must constantly be noted. A version of the Apocryphon of John uses the term Metropator very frequently as an androgynous definition of the first emanation, the Ennoia. However, in at least two passages the context in fact suggests the association of the Metropator with the supreme light God and Father of the universe.[312] Although the fact that the Coptic text has no punctuation makes the relationship difficult to establish, these passages serve Elaine Pagels' interests more than the Metropator passage which she quotes. So one is surprised that Pagels does not refer to them. But be this as it may, individual androgynous statements about the supreme God of the Gnostics do not stand the image on its head, and in myth, too, the feminine element is constantly faced with the alternative of either abandoning its femininity or producing disaster.

Fallen Sophia

The creator God is, as Pagels argues, not without a touch of gloating, 'castigated for his arrogance – nearly always by a superior feminine power.'[313] But Pagels does not say clearly enough that this creator God, whom the reader involuntarily imagines as being the God of the Christian Bible, is not identical with the Unimaginable, the pure light, and thus the supreme God of the Gnostics. By contrast the Gnostic creator of the world is the result of a fall of Sophia, one of the emanations: called Yaldabaoth or demiurge, he is regarded as being covetous and evil. Through blindness and rebellion against the light world above he has created the world, our world, and therefore there can be no good in it. Such statements as that the creator of the world is an evil demiurge, that all that is created thus comes from an evil power and is out to trap humanity or its divine spirit-self in matter, stand in sharp contrast to the Christian conception of God as supreme good and creation as the good creation of God. But let us allow the myth once again to speak for itself. As the last of the many divine emanations Sophia, Wisdom, also belongs to the upper world of light. All emanations stand in a relationship of praise to the true light.[314] But the fall began:

> And the Sophia of the Epinoia, being an aeon, conceived a thought from herself with the reflection of the invisible Spirit and foreknowledge. She wanted to bring forth a likeness out of herself without the consent of the Spirit – he had not approved – and without her consort and without his consideration. And though her maleness had not approved and she had not found her agreement, and she had thought without the consent of the Spirit and the knowledge of her agreement, (yet) she brought forth... And a thing came out of her which was imperfect and different from her appearance because she had created it without her consort. And it was dissimilar to the likeness of its mother for it has another form.[315]

And she saw the consequence of her desire, it had changed into a form of a lion-faced serpent... She cast it away from her, outside that place, that no one of the immortal ones might see it, for she had created it in ignorance. And she surrounded it with a luminous cloud, and she placed a throne in the middle of the cloud that no one might see it except the holy Spirit who is called the mother of the living. And she called his name Yaldabaoth. This is the first archon who took a great power from his mother. And he removed himself from her... He became strong... and he joined with his madness which is in him and begot authorities for himself.[316]

The realm of Yaldabaoth is the realm of darkness, folly and desire. He creates the planets, and rules over heaven (the worlds of heaven), chaos and the underworld.[317] 'But he gave them nothing of the pure light that is the power that he had taken from his mother. Therefore he was Lord over them because of the glory of the light of the power which is in him from the mother. Therefore he called himself God over them, in that he rebelled against his substance from which he had come forth.'[318] Meanwhile Sophia weeps over her mistake, which consisted in the fact that she wanted to produce from herself a notion which was as self-active, alone and autonomous in authority as the Ineffable, the pure light. So she mistook her status and forgot that she herself was an emanation of the Most High. But her pair, the Spirit, came down, 'to correct her deficiency'.[319]

In the shorter version of the Apocryphon of John a further theme is the desire which then becomes a characteristic of Yaldabaoth: 'But she did not find her consort when she began to produce it without the consent of the pneuma (= Spirit) and without her own consort by emanating because of the sensual desire within her.'[320] As a result, here too Yaldabaoth makes an archon of his own in the image of the incorruptible aeons, a kind of counter-world with 360 kinds of angels who all take their names from envy and wrath. Yaldabaoth says to his angels: 'I am a jealous God, there is none beside me.' And the text interprets: 'But by announcing this he indicated to the angels who attended to him that there exists another God, for if there were no other one, of whom would he be jealous?'[321] Here Yaldabaoth is seen as the God of the Old Testament.

In a later work, the Pistis Sophia, which indulges in excessive heavenly speculations and already has features of a 'Gnosticism grown old',[322] Jesus reveals to his disciples his experiences on his journey through the aeons. On it he meets Sophia, who sits all alone beneath the thirteenth aeon and laments because she is not accepted in the aeon. The reason:

> It happened while the Pistis Sophia was in the thirteenth of the aeons in the place of all her brothers the invisibles, namely twenty-four emanations of the great invisible... the Pistis Sophia looked to the height. She saw the light of the veil of the treasury of the light and she desired to go to that place and she could not prevail to go to that place. But she ceased doing the mystery of the thirteenth aeon... But she praised the light, the height. It happened therefore while she was hymning the praise of the height all the rulers who were in the twelve aeons heard her, because she ceased from their mysteries and because she wished to go to the height and be above all.[323]

Now Authades, one of the triple powers, who had also become disobedient through a refusal to emanate his power, grew angry like the archons and pestered Pistis Sophia: 'And he emanated a great power with the face of a lion... and sent it to the places below... that they should waylay the Pistis Sophia there and take away her power from her.'[324] There Pistis Sophia sees the power with the lion's face, is deceived, and believes that the light which she sees is identical with the light from the heights; from this light she hopes to gain power to ascend the heights again: 'I will go to that place without my consort and make myself some aeons of light so that I am able to go to the light of lights.'[325] Hardly has she descended than the emanations of the Authades surround her, absorb the light from her and turn the material shell into chaos. So she herself becomes an archon with a lion's face who sits in chaos and is called Yaldabaoth, identical with the demiurge whom she produced.[326] The Gnostic Ptolemaeus, who was active as a pupil of Valentinus at the end of the first and beginning of the second centuries,[327] has a variant of the fall of Sophia in which there is a division between an upper and a lower Sophia: '...Sophia hurled herself forwards and became the victim of Pathos (= passion) without the protection of her consort Theletos (= what is willed)... In so doing Sophia feigned love, but in truth this was done through audacity, because she could not have such inward communion with the perfect Father (= the supreme ineffable God) as she had with the Nous (= reason). Now Pathos is the search for the Father.'[328] This, of course, is an impossible undertaking, because the depth and unfathomability of the Father sets a limit (Horos) to her. Thereupon she bears an amorphous being which has manifest imperfections, so she attempts to hide it. In her despair she turns imploringly to the Father who separates Sophia from Pathos and restores her own consort; she is taken back into the pleroma (fullness) as the upper Sophia, and covetousness is expelled from the pleroma to the place of shadows. The upper Christ, in common with the holy Spirit, who emanated from the supreme God to heal the fall of Sophia, descends to the shadow and leaves behind to covetousness 'a certain aroma of immorality (= the lower Sophia in the duality of matter and light)'.[329]

From the 'return to that which had given her life (= Christ)' there now derives the demiurge, who is called Metropator (!) (= Mother/Father), Fatherless or Father because he is the Father and God of all beings outside the Pleroma, the creator of all psychical and hylic beings. 'He brought forth an earth without knowing the earth.'[330] He believed he was the only God and had this erroneous faith proclaimed by the prophets.[331] The 'title' Metropator is therefore given not only to the emanations of God but also to the demiurge, but because of his covetousness it has negative connotations.

An example from the Hypostasis of the Archons rounds off the picture.[332] Here the demiurge is the great one who rules over the powers of darkness. Blinded by power, folly and arrogance, he says: 'I am God and there is no one beside me.' And the text explains: 'So he sinned against the all. These his words arose to the Incorruptible and the Incorruptible said: You are wrong, Samael, God of the blind.'[333] Here, too, the fall of Sophia is described as an attempt to emanate without her pair and independently to produce an image of the All. The consequence is that a shadow comes between the light and the lower regions, intensifies into matter – a miscarriage of Sophia, a beast in the form of a lion, arrogant and androgynous. In order to cause the worst possible hindrance to this demiurge, who is also called Samael or

Saklas, Sophia stretches out her finger to illuminate matter with light. In this way the demiurge now has power enough to create heaven and earth, a counter-world to the light world of the pleroma, in which portions of light have, however, been trapped as a result of the finger of Sophia.[334]

The selection of motives

The mythical figure of Sophia thus remains ambivalent: through her revolt against the supreme God, and her covetousness, she is the cause of the Fall; through her share in the light she is part of the pleroma and a divine being. That is all too reminiscent of the ambivalence of evil lust and holy aura, of whore and saint, of Eve and Mary, which is usually attributed to the woman.

So what has been gained here as an alternative to the stereotyped Christian clichés of femininity? As already with the basic questions about the anthropology of Gnosticism, Pagels' motive-historical method also does not seem very productive in relation to the question of the androgynous God and his emanations, thought of as being feminine. Thus it is the great deficiency of her book that nowhere does she depict the Gnostic myth in its overall context, but again presents individual themes which produce a new distinctive context when the reader does not (or cannot) take the trouble to gain insight into the sources. When Pagels speaks of 'God' who is thought of as androgynous in Gnosticism and called Metropator, within the Gnostic myth the figure to whom she refers is the demiurge, a miscarriage of Sophia. He is ignorant, arrogant, evil and covetous; he creates our world as a counter-world to the aeons of the pleroma and is therefore concerned to collect all the light, from which he derives his power. To that end he imprisons light in matter by creating human beings. For Gnosticism this demiurge is identical with the biblical creator God, and to this degree Pagels is already right when she says that the Gnostics see the biblical God in masculine-feminine duality. However, if one bears in mind the overall context of the Gnostic myth, the worthlessness of those androgynous conceptions for any feminist interest becomes evident. They exclusively have negative connotations! Sophia is certainly superior to the demiurge God, but she is merely one of the emanations of the highest light-God and the occasion of a fall from which the world of darkness, death, ignorance and covetousness comes into being – again it is a feminine being which provokes all this disaster. Finally eroticism, which is what determines the relationship of the sexes in this world, is interpreted in exclusively negative terms as covetousness and as the consequence of a fall.

Feminist interest is right when it questions the millennia-old defamations of the feminine and of women; but it does not help women where it combines this interest with an offence against historical honesty. On the contrary, it harms them, because it is easy for the opposition to repudiate the selected 'facts' and thus also to dislocate the interest. Whereas male scholars usually follow the model 'because what may not be, cannot be', women practise the principle, 'because what cannot be must definitely be'. The one is not better than the other.

Now Pagels is well aware that the various Gnostic texts display a large number of contradictions and are in no way a unity, and she is also honest enough to mention passages in which the feminine is spoken of in disparaging categories. However, she regards such texts as exceptions.[335] Thus the Gospel of Thomas, a text of genuine Christian Gnosticism (probably from the third century) which the Nag Hammadi discovery has made available in its entirety, says: 'Simon Peter said to the disciples: Mary (Magdalene) must depart from us, for women are not worthy of life. Jesus said: Behold, I will take her to make her male, so that she too becomes a living spirit who is like you men. For any woman who makes herself male will enter the kingdom of heaven.'[336] Mary Magdalene is worthy to enter heaven, but on condition that she becomes what the disciples already are by virtue of their sex, namely male.

From the Book of Thomas the Contender,[337] which is also one of the Christian Gnostic finds from Nag Hammadi dating from the time of the Gospel of Thomas, Pagels quotes the sentence. 'Woe to you who love intimacy with womankind, and polluted intercourse with it!'[338] The Paraphrase of Shem, a popular Gnostic text from the second century, which has only a very superficial relationship to Christian conceptions, teaches us that nature 'turned her dark vagina and cast from her the power of fire, which was with her from the beginning, through the practice of darkness'.[339] And in the Nag Hammadi text 'The Dialogue of the Redeemer'[340] Jesus admonishes his disciples 'to pray at a place where there is no woman' and 'to destroy the works of femininity'.[341]

This ascetical theme is attested over centuries and therefore cannot be the exception, as Pagels thinks. At all events, it is the consequence of a myth which sees the world as the creation of a foolish and sexually covetous demiurge. Ambivalence over femininity can be found in orthodox Christian literature just as in Gnostic literature; so in what does Gnostic superiority consist? In the end one must grant the orthodox Christians that their canon does not contain such disparaging statements about the feminine, even as the exception. Pagels attempts to excuse the Gnostics with the argument that they are not speaking out against women but against the 'power of sexuality'.[342] But what advantage is there for the feminist interest again to separate women from their sexuality, in order to protect them from defamation as individuals? The interest of the Gnostics in such a separation is understandable; they are ascetics. So the important thing will be what emerges from their life-style and how this relates to the orthopraxy of the Christian church communities of the time.

CHAPTER SEVEN

The Conflicts of the Third Generation

Asceticism of the elect

The Gnostic myth represents the sexual differentiation of human beings, which is experienced in desire as a polar tension, as the result of a fall.[343] Sexuality and procreation are therefore dirty. In the Apocryphon of John, which I have already cited several times, Yaldabaoth creates the first man Adam. In order to heal the deficiency of Sophia and to put a brake on the disaster once it has been started, Sophia as mother breathes the pneuma (= spirit) into human beings so that from then on they bear within themselves sparks of light of which the archons are envious. The archons are now after the light, and in order to draw it out from Adam they create – Eve. The tree of which both human beings finally eat is forbidden them by the demiurge God, who has no interest in human beings gaining knowlege (= gnosis) from this tree. The serpent now shows them 'the procreation from desire which is dirty'.[344] When Yaldabaoth sees the virgin Eve he wants to have offspring from her: he 'sullies' her and thus begets Yave (= Yahweh) and Eloim. 'Now up to the present day sexual intercourse continued due to the chief archon. And he placed sexual desire in her who belongs to Adam. And they produced through intercourse the copies of their bodies...'[345] Since for the Gnostics the body and thus human sexuality are matter which is hostile to God, nothing which has anything to do with corporeality can be assessed in a positive way; on the contrary, the spirit-self must keep itself untouched by matter, detach itself from it in order to free itself. The Gnostics who understood themselves to be elect practised sexual aceticism.[346] Anyone who had committed the mistake of procreating during his days on earth had first, after a migration of souls, to be incarnated in a new existence in order to receive a chance of higher knowledge.[347] Pagels declares such asceticism to be an extremist attitude – and so another exception?[348]

Ascetical practice is attested in many Gnostic texts. The church father Irenaeus wrote of the Gnostic Satornilus:[349] 'He taught that the redeemer is unborn, incorporeal, without a form and only apparently man...[350] Marrying and begetting come from Satan...[351] Numerous followers of Satornilus also abstained from animal food and led many astray by hypocritical continence of such a kind.'[352] And on the teaching of Basilides, who worked as a contemporary of Valentinus in Alexandria in Egypt and similarly formed a school and gathered followers around him, Clement of Alexandria writes:[353] 'The followers of Basilides say that when the apostles asked whether it was not better not to marry, the Lord replied: "Not all can receive this saying; there are some eunuchs who are so from their birth, others are so of necessity" (Matt.12.11-12). And their explanation of this saying is roughly as follows: Some men, from their birth, have a natural sense of repulsion from a woman; and those who are naturally constituted do well not to marry... But those who for the sake of the eternal kingdom have made themselves eunuchs derive this idea, they say, from a wish to avoid the distractions involved in marriage, because they are afraid of having to waste time in providing for the necessities of life... Human nature has some wants which are necessary and natural, and others which are only natural. To be clothed is necessary and natural; sexual intercourse is natural but not necessary.'[354]

The Gospel of Thomas[355] contains a series of sayings which seem to indicate asceticism. Alluding to the break-up of the original unity of the syzygies or the origin of sexual differentiation it says: 'On the day when you were one you became two.'[356] 'When you make the two one, and when you make the inside like the outside and the outside like the inside, and the above like the below, and when you make the male and the female one and the same, so that the male not be male nor the female female... then you will enter the kingdom.'[357] 'Whoever has come to understand the world has found (only) a corpse, and whoever has found a corpse is superior to the world.'[358] Equally characteristic of the abolition of sexual differentiation in human beings is the shift in meaning in the text of Luke 11.27-28, where a woman from the people praises the body and breasts of the mother of Jesus and Jesus rejects this with the words 'Blessed are those who hear the word of God.' In the Gospel of Thomas we read: 'Blessed are the womb which has not conceived and the breasts which have not given milk.'[359] Therefore it is consistent when Jesus must and will make Mary Magdalene male so that she can become a living spirit[360] – here too the polarity of the sexes is transcended.

According to the Gospel of Philip the pneumatic whose spirit-self enters upon the journey into the pleroma is given a password which indicates that he is an initiate and enlightened: 'I have recognized myself and gathered myself together from all sides and have not sown children to the Archon but have uprooted his roots... But if it should prove that it (= soul/spirit-self) has born a son, it is kept beneath.'[361]

The sayings about ascetical practice are associated with the repudiation of libertinistic praxis on the part of the Gnostics.[362] The ambivalence or interchangeability of both attitudes is part of the popular verdict on Gnosticism which the church fathers also adopt. In the Gnostic writings themselves there is just one passage in which such a charge of libertinism is taken up by the Gnostics and at the same time rejected. In the Pistis Sophia, one of the disciples, Thomas, says: 'We have heard that there are some upon earth who take the sperm of the male with the menstrual blood of the women and put them in a dish of lentils and eat it, saying, We believe in Esau and Jacob. Is that right or not?' Jesus answers: 'This sin surpasses every sin and every unlawfulness.'[363]

So if there were such and similar practices in Gnostic circles, they were sharply rejected by other Gnostics. But it is also possible that this was an answer to calumniations above all by orthodox Christians. All the other evidence about alleged libertine practice among the Gnostics can be attributed to the church fathers and thus belongs in the literary genre of polemic against the heretics, which carries little credibility. Above all Epiphanius, Bishop on Cyprus, had been a member of a Gnostic group in Egypt for a while,[364] and is aware from this period of real abominations among these people: the Gnostics had all women in common, in their cultic associations they practised gluttony in order to unite themselves sexually. Epiphanius mentions a similar theme to the

Pistis Sophia: men and women take male sperm in their hands, look up to heaven, and pray for acceptance of the gift, the body of Christ. They eat the menstrual blood of women and call it the blood of Christ. If a wife nevertheless becomes pregnant because the *coitus interruptus* has failed they tear out the embryo, stamp on it, season it, and make everyone eat it.[365] Something similar appears in the Gnostic writing 'Questions of Mary' which is handed down only by Epiphanius, the Mary being Mary Magdalene:[366] Jesus took Mary with him on the mountain to pray with her, brought forth a woman from his side, began to unite with her and then collected his seed as a sacrificial gift.[367]

However, the fact that Epiphanius was a convert, who like so many converts tried where possible to dissociate himself from his former life, combined with the fact that he was one of the most rabid heresy hunters and denounced members of the church community who were suspected of Gnosticism, suggests that he was not a very moderate character – in his judgments either. So such statements must be treated with great care. The heresy-hunting of all times and groups contains the charge of unbridled lust, since there are those who evidently cannot imagine that people who put forward false teaching nevertheless lead respectable lives. Heresy-hunting follows a kind of progression:[368] an attempt at conversion; isolation (excommunication); disparagement, above all in sexual matters; a reversal of views; and finally persecution, trial and execution.[369] 'Perhaps there were libertinist Gnostics, perhaps they practised these deviations out of their Gnostic concern for freedom – but it would not be characteristic of Gnosticism, nor is there credible evidence of it in our sources. Where the Gnostic deviates from the ethical norm, so far as we know it always happens in the direction of asceticism.'[370] 'Quite apart from the scurrilous gossip that went the rounds, the view of the church fathers comes about because they could not imagine how any good, namely morality, could be found among the devil and his sons, namely the heretics.'[371]

'He kissed her on the mouth'

In some groups of Valentinians[372] the Sophia myth corresponded to the rite of the nuptial chamber, which was regarded as a sacrament of redemption: 'Some of them prepare a nuptial chamber and perform an initiation with certain formulae on those who are to be introduced to the mystery, and they call this event "spiritual marriage" in imitation of the syzygies above.'[373] As the association of male and female in pairs in the syzygies of the pleroma represents the transcending of sexual polarity and is thought to be free of any sexual desire, the spiritualization of the difference of sexes in the sacrament of the nuptial chamber corresponds to it. So we also read in the Gospel of Philip: 'Had the woman not separated from the man' (i.e. had the syzygy not been done away with by the fall), 'it would not die along with the man. This separation became the beginning of death. For that reason, because of the separation which had come about from the beginning, Christ can rise again and unite the two and give life to those who have died in the separation and reunite them.'[374]

The marriage of the world is a pollution, spotless marriage a true mystery. 'It is not fleshly, but pure; it does not belong to the desire but to the will.' It does not belong to darkness but to the light. The sign of this sacrament is the kiss.[375] The mystery of the nuptial chamber is also called 'a copy' (of the syzygies above). That no actual sexual intercourse is involved in it emerges finally from the following passage: 'No one will be able to have the audacity to go to the man or the woman. They (the archons) can no longer lay hold of the one who has come forth from the world...'[376] Thus anyone who has received the sacrament of the nuptial chamber is free from matter, so that the evil archons can no longer touch him if the spirit-self, the inner spark of light, enters upon the journey into the pleroma.[377]

In this symbolic context Mary Magdalene now takes on her specifically Gnostic significance. She plays a striking central role in Gnostic writings, something else that Elaine Pagels brings out and exploits for her feminist interest.[378] Mary asks Jesus the most questions: of forty-six questions from the disciples in the Pistis Sophia, thirty-nine come from Mary.[379] The reaction follows promptly: 'Peter said: My Lord, let the women cease from asking questions, that we may ask questions too.' And Jesus says to the women: 'Give your male brethren the opportunity, that they too may ask.'[380]

Mary Magdalene also plays a decisive role in the writing

'Questions of Mary' which I have already mentioned, though we have this work not in an original text but only as handed down by the heresy-hunter Epiphanius,[381] and in the 'Gospel according to Mary' from Nag Hammadi (second century), which also differs from it in content;[382] again Mary Magdalene emerges in a very dominant way among the questioning disciples. She also comforts the disciples and continually coaxes them out of their indecision. The disciples also complain that Jesus prefers her and they mistrust what she says. That reduces Mary to despair. But Levi defends her and says: 'But if the Redeemer has made her worthy, who are you (he means Peter again) to reject her? Surely the Redeemer knows her full well. For that reason he loved her more than us.'[383]

Mary also makes an appearance in the Gospel of Philip, as the 'consort of the Saviour'. 'The Saviour loved Mary Magdalene more than all the disciples. And he often kissed her on the mouth.'[384] That Mary was the closest woman companion of Jesus emerges from the text of Luke 8.1-3. In the Gnostic texts she therefore becomes a consort of Jesus, but in a different sense from that which erotic romantic fantasy might assume.[385] Just as the redeemer, as an emanation of the supreme Gnostic God, belongs to the light world and therefore has nothing to do with the world of Archons, so too Mary is a light-being of the pleroma. She is bound to Jesus in the syzygy and is therefore more than the disciples: 'Mary is his sister and his mother and his consort.'[386] Therefore she can also instruct the disciples, like Jesus does as revealer of gnosis.[387] In the Gospel of Philip she is therefore logically identified with Sophia: 'Sophia who is called the "unfruitful", she is the mother of the angels and the consort of Christ is Mary Magdalene... The other women (disciples) saw how he loved Mary. They said to him: Why do you love her more than all of us? The Soter (= Saviour) answered and said to them: Why do I not love you as her?'[388] Only the pneumatic knows the answer: because she is his pair, because he forms the heavenly syzygy with her. The kiss on the mouth represents the association with the sacrament of the nuptial chamber and may not be understood as 'fleshly practice'. Thus the sacred marriage represents the marriage of the spirit-self in human beings with the pleroma; the spark of light returns whence it came; the part fuses with the whole.

On close inspection the theories of Elaine Pagels do not stand up: Gnosticism does not present a mother god nor is there in the Gnostic communities any undisputed affirmation of natural human sexuality. A woman is accepted as a sexless being, indeed as a 'man'.

Women and heresy

On the other hand there is no question that the involvement of women in the Gnostic communities was even greater than that of men.[389] The church father Irenaeus notes this with special consternation and even attributes the fact to the attraction of heresy and the ease with which women can be led astray.[390] Now not only did the Gnostic mission turn predominantly to women, but so too did the orthodox Christian mission.[391] Pagan polemic held that against the Christians;[392] and just as the Gentiles accused the Christians, so later the Christians accused the Gnostics that women in the community did not act with the necessary restraint.

That women were fond of joining heretical movements is also a common feature of the mediaeval history of heresy. 'From the Montanist movement on, the history of enthusiasm is largely a history of female emancipation, and it is not a reassuring one.'[393] But why is that so?

Usually the tendency of women to prefer heretical groups is interpreted as a moral or 'natural weakness of women', which caused the battle against heresy to be associated with the battle against women, so that the one was justified by the other – in the service of what interests is quite clear. A somewhat more sober interpretation in terms of social psychology brings other aspects critical of orthodoxy to light: 'The central conception of the free thinker, self-deification, had a predominantly compensatory function, for on entering the sect the believers appropriated all those rights that they did not possess and so ascended from an utter lack of rights to supreme divinity.'[394] 'People who are completely alienated from society escape its contradictions and their despair by entrusting themselves fully to a new symbolic order... In mediaeval Christian society this means above all the repudiation of Christian values and Christian ritual.'[395] *Mutatis mutandis* this verdict on the Middle Ages can also be applied to the first centuries. The early Christian communities as they are presented to us above all through the mirror of the letters of Paul at first testify to a very balanced role for women; ultimately the Christians are rightly understood as a heretical group within Judaism. As I have already shown, this heretical charismatic movement of Christians gradually adapted to society. Pagan criticism at any rate played some part in this development, a criticism which was directed against Christianity as a religion of women. Thus the pagan Celsus, who has been called a second-century Voltaire and whose arguments against Christianity have to be reconstructed from the writings of his contemporary the church father Origen, finds malicious words: '...so it is clear that they will and can convince only the simple and lowly and those without understanding and slaves and women and children... And if they so wish they must go with the women and the children who play with them into the women's room or the cobbler's or the fuller's so that these may gain perfection and they may convince them by saying this.'[396] Over against that social adaptation always means gaining respect in public and therefore avoiding offence in public by again becoming familiar with the 'wisdom of the world' and thus taking the wind out of the sails of pagan critics by a well-ordered Christian home.

It is not surprising that women joined groups which promised them value and esteem before God and men. That this high estimation of women evidently goes hand in hand with the repudiation of 'bourgeois' social norms does not tell against women, but points to the guilt and deficiency of human beings and structures. Where a church does not integrate women with all their gifts into community life in accordance with the criterion of the beginnings attested in the canon, in the same way as it does men, it is laying the foundation for the next exodus of heretics. Heresies do not emerge by chance; they are also provoked. Feminist theology today is a clear warning signal.[397]

This can be 'learned' from the history of Gnosticism, which is not a genuinely Christian belief, far less a better Christianity, as Elaine Pagels thinks: it can be learned, precisely because Gnosticism is a heresy. It seems likely that women felt themselves attracted by Gnostic communities since there were elements in them which Christian orthodoxy had already abandoned, or was on the point of abandoning under the pressure of controversy with the threat posed by heresy. In this reciprocal process the tendency to social adaptation and consolidation in the mainstream church received vigorous support.

It is hard to reconstruct the community life of the Gnostics on the basis of the source material. What can be grasped is astonishing enough. The sorrow of the orthodox was the women's delight: 'And even the heretical women, how cheeky and arrogant they are! They submit to learning, they dispute, they perform exorcisms, promise healings, and perhaps even baptize.'[398] The author of these lines, Tertullian before his Montanist period, plays down the Gnostic praxis with his 'perhaps', for it was known that women had baptized in Gnostic communities, and that is hardly likely to have escaped Tertullian.[399] It is said of the Marcusians, a tendency among the Valentinians,[400] that women had made the eucharistic offerings: 'Then again he (Marcus) gives the women cups with mixed wine and commands (the word 'command' is anti-Gnostic polemic) them to say the thanksgiving in his presence.'[401] Marcus also said to women, 'Open your mouth and prophesy!'[402] If a woman thinks that she cannot, he insists: 'Open your mouth and say whatever you want and you will prophesy.'[403]

There is a good deal of evidence in Gnosticism for prophetesses, like Maximilla and Priscilla among the Montanists, whom Tertullian joined at a late stage,[404] and Philumene, who communicated revelations to Apelles, a pupil of Marcion,[405] or Marcellina, a representative of the Carpocratians.[406]

Nevertheless, if one wants to identify such practice with contemporary ideas about the emancipation of women one will be mistaken about the intentions of Gnosticism. 'Gnosticism has no more ideas about social reform than the Christianity of the church. Through its negation of any secular order, however, Gnosticism loses its conservative character.'[407] This apt comment by Heinrich Kraft, who has investigated Gnostic community life, recalls the beginnings of Christianity. But the differences also emerge. For the Gnostics, the body as matter and thus the whole social order belongs to the kingdom of the evil archons. Therefore social roles are not worth anything; all that matters is gnosis, the knowledge that the spirit-self of man, whether male or female, derives from the light world of the pleroma and seeks to return there. The renunciation of charitable activity and the anti-hierarchical structures of the community are due to the negation of the world and asceticism as rebellion against the powers of darkness. These two motives cannot be separated, however much we might like to attempt that.[408]

Another not very desirable motive – in terms of today's norms – which also cannot be denied in the case of the Gnostics, is their sense of being an élite. That is true on the one hand over against the orthodox Christians. In the Tripartite Tractate[409] there is talk of the pneumatics as the 'children of the Father', all with equal status, and the ordinary Christians and descendants of the demiurge are free of the desire to rule: they want 'to command one another, outrivalling one another in their empty ambition, each one imagining that he is superior to the others...'[410]

However, the sense among the pneumatics of being an élite has an internal effect on the members of the Gnostic community, for only the pneumatics, the elect, are equal to one another. The psychics and the hylics are clearly lower down in the hierarchy. A vivid example of this is offered by Manichaeism, which was founded by the Persian Mani, who claimed to be an apostle of Jesus Christ. It spread with great success: missionary journeys took Mani to China and his teaching was carried as far as Spain.[411] Among Manichaeans the elect occupied themselves with good works and redemption: they did not practise agriculture, and indeed regarded this as reprehensible, since the life of plants and trees may not be violated. Anyone who practises agriculture is in one sense a murderer. The elect do not even pick fruit, 'but wait until these things are brought for their use by their hearers... thus – considered from the standpoint of their own vain doctrine – they live by so many and great murders committed by others.'[412] So their hearers, who feed the elect, are guilty[413] and must ask for forgiveness for this guilt, as emerges from the Manichaean penitential rules.[414] One can hardly talk here of a model of social justice; indeed all social affairs belong in the sphere of matter, which is hostile to God.

If we connect these remarks once again with the question of women, again with Heinrich Kraft it may be said; 'Only among the Gnostics is it possible for the tasks of a priest to be performed by women, only where the flesh no longer has any quality with sacral consequences... Rather, only the human being who is asexual is capable of redemption. Priesthood and hierurgy is a secular order: here more is involved.'[415] What Kraft says also applies to Gnosticism. The critical question is, must that be? Is the equal estimation of women necessarily connected with disparagement of the body and the ascetical practices that go with that disparagement? History seems to confirm this, especially if, to conclude with, we once again look back at the New Testament, at the texts of the third generation.

Conservatism becomes established

The Pastoral Epistles, I and II Timothy and Titus, were written about a generation after Paul, at the beginning of the second century. From their style and content it can be demonstrated that despite what is said in the prescript Paul is not the author, and Timothy and Titus, Paul's two most important fellow-workers, cannot be the recipients. The three works are 'pastoral letters', addressed by a pastor to the flock, and give instructions about leading the community. A defence[416] against the Gnostic heresy stands in the foreground: 'O Timothy... avoid the godless chatter and contradictions of what is falsely called knowledge (*gnosis*)...' (I Tim.6.20). The three pastoral letters attempt to consolidate the Christian communities against the Gnostic temptation through a fixed church order, 'sound' doctrine and an assured ethic for everyday use.[417] Therefore they are really addressed to the whole church.

Whereas the letters of Paul still gave evidence of the free working of charismata, the gifts of the Spirit, which was attested in the communities, a generation later the ordering of ministries, liturgy and the household stand at the centre. Ministries are not described in the Pastoral Epistles but presupposed, and characteristically are mentioned in the 'teaching of obligations in tabular form'.[418] It is said of the bishop (*episcopos*) that he must be above reproach, husband of only one wife, sober, wise, skilled in teaching: he is not to be devoted to wine; he is to be hospitable and not avaricious; above all he is to look after his own house well and see that his children are obedient, since, the conclusion goes, anyone who cannot look after his own house will not be able to look after the community. A new convert is not suited to be a bishop, as new converts have the reputation of being conceited and pround. The reason for such high moral demands is given at the end of the section: the bishop must have a good reputation among those outside, namely the non-Christians (II Tim.3.1-7). This is possible only if the moral criteria and behaviour of the ministers of the Christian community are adapted to the moral ideas which are also accepted outside the community, whereas both for Jesus and his followers, as for the initial period of the formation of the community, the criteria in this area differ from what is usual elsewhere in the world.

The degree to which the role and assessment of women has changed in these conditions is evident from the continuation of the text in I Timothy. Of behaviour in worship it is said: 'I desire then that in every place the men should pray, lifting holy hands without anger or quarrelling; also that women should adorn themselves modestly and sensibly in seemly apparel, not with braided hair or gold or pearls or costly attire but by good deeds, as befits women who profess religion. Let a woman learn in silence with all submissiveness. I permit no woman to teach or to have authority over men; she is to keep silent. For Adam was not deceived, but the woman was deceived and became a transgressor. Yet woman will be saved through bearing children, if she continues in faith and love and holiness, with modesty' (I Tim.2.8-15).

This is also the context of the famous passage which requires women to be silent in the community assembly and which erroneously is still attributed to Paul: 'As in all the churches of the saints, the women should keep silence in the churches. For they are not permitted to speak, but should be subordinate, as even the law says. If there is anything they desire to know, let them ask their husbands at home. For it is shameful for a woman to speak in church. What! Did the word of God originate with you, or are you the only ones it has reached?' (I Cor.14.33b-36). These verses are an insertion from the time and attitude of the Pastoral Epistles, as Paul himself nowhere warns against the public appearance of women in the community (cf. I Cor.11.4,5 or the attitude of Paul to the women fellow workers in the various communities).[419] Nowhere in his letters does Paul demand that women should be subordinate, nor does the appeal to the Jewish law correspond to Paul's theology, according to which this law was ended by Jesus Christ. In addition there is a literary-critical argument. If one goes on reading the text from I Cor.14.33a to v.37 there is no sense of a gap. The keywords prophecy, silence and subordination from the section v.26-33a were taken as an occasion by a later redactor for introducing his 'correction', though they stand in a completely different context.[420]

Prophetic speech in assemblies, still attested as a gift of the spirit to both women and men among communities at the time of Paul, no longer appears a generation later. In addition to the office of bishop the Pastoral Epistles also speak of the office of presbyter, who are admonished along the same lines as the bishops (I Tim.5.17-19; Titus 1.5f.), and the ministry of deacons (I Tim.3.8-13). Verse 11 is striking in this connection: 'The women likewise must be serious, no slanderers, but temperate, faithful in all things.' Are the women mentioned here the wives of the deacons, which is what many translations opt for, or is this the office of deacon, which we have already come across in connection with Phoebe?[421] It is hard to make a firm decision because of the brevity of the text, but there are many arguments in favour of thinking that these are deacons: no wives are mentioned in connection with other ministries, the women appear in the context of rules about ministers, the admonitions fit those to the deacons and finally the text speaks of 'women' and not of 'their wives'.[422] It follows from this that the office of woman deacon lasted down to the third generation,[423] but is not important enough to the author of the Pastoral Epistles for him to want to devote more than this one sentence to it.

Instead, a new 'office' for women appears, the 'office' of widow, though this is tied to strict conditions (I Tim.5.3-16). Texts from the Old Testament already show how hard was the lot of widows without means. Injustice against widows and the way in which they were exploited is a fixed ingredient of prophetic criticism (cf. e.g. Isa.1.23; 10.2; Jer.5.28; 7.6; Ezek.22.7). The Christian community made the care of widows its task. In this text 'real widows' are distinguished for those who have children, nephews and nieces or other relations who have a Christian duty to care for their widows (I Tim.5.4,8,16). Real widows must also be more than sixty (v.9), since younger women are suspected of lasciviousness (vv.11-12). The moral conditions are also spelt out in detail: the widow must, of course, be respectable and have been the wife of only one husband; she should have brought up children, practised hospitality (including the service of footwashing, which otherwise was only performed by slaves) and must generally be proven in charitable activity of all kinds (vv.7-10). The real widow is completely alone, puts all her hope in God and prays day and night (v.5). It is here that her quasi-ministerial functions lie.[424] And to be entrusted with this ministry which includes being cared for by the community, she needs to make a public vow (v.12).

So both old and young women have their relevant duties. All women are 'to be reverent in behaviour, not to be slanderers or slaves to drink; they are to teach what is good, and so train the young women to love their husbands and children, to be sensible, chaste, domestic, kind, and submissive to their husbands, that the word of God be not discredited' (Titus 2.3-5).

There were catalogues of duties at the end of the first and beginning of the second century not only for ministers in the community but also for the household, in so-called house tables. The oldest house table appears in Colossians (3.18-4.1); there is an extended version in Ephesians, which is later, but in literary terms that is dependent on Colossians (5.22-6.9).

Like the Pastorals, these two letters are pseudepigrapha, i.e. texts deliberately but inappropriately attributed to Paul. Here too the authority of the apostle is used to convey important matters to the Christian communities (and not just those in Colossae and Ephesus). The letter to the Ephesians, which was written at the end of the first or the beginning of the second century and after Colossians, is concerned with the unity of the church, while Colossians combats heresies (Gnostic heresies).

In both texts women are enjoined to be subservient to their husbands: the reason given is that of a general custom, 'as is seemly' (Col.3.18). Ephesians also presupposes that the husband is 'the head of the wife' (5.23). Accordingly the attitude of women towards their husbands is characterized by the term 'fear' (Eph.5.33).

Husbands, by contrast, are admonished to love their wives.[425] In this context the church does not refer to a universal custom, because the love of husbands towards wives was not a very widespread maxim compared with the subordination of wives to their husbands. However, even in the literature of non-Christian antiquity there are texts which define the relationship between the married couple in precisely the same way as the two New Testament house tables just mentioned. Thus for example Plutarch, the first-century philosopher and writer, writes: 'As long as they (the wives) are subordinate to their husbands, they deserve praise... But the husband must not rule over his wife like a despot over his property, but like the soul over the body – full of compassion and growing together with her in love.'[426] Certainly 'the option for a "subordination" of women controlled by the "love" of their husbands was not one that could be taken for granted'.[427] There were then and there are now many worst things, against the background of which Plutarch and the house tables look like paradise. Some women have already sighed on reading these texts, 'If only men did behave like that, subordination would be worth it.' However, these texts are not to be measured by the criterion of a betrayal of humanity, but represent a development in the Christian communities. 1. From the Jesus tradition on there was criticism of any form of power; in view of the kingdom of God the important thing was service, and therefore it was unnecessary to restrain the *patria potestas*. 2. What the Christians around the turn of the century took over with the house tables is an ancient pagan model which served the economy of the household. Here 'it was a matter of the functioning of economic and social efforts', which remained fruitless unless the married couple and the other members of the house were in harmony.[428] This wisdom is still valid and not bound to the conditions of the Christian creed. So the Christians of that time adapted to social reality. The motive can be taken to be that expressed in I Tim.3.7 in connection with the duties of ministers: the respect of those who are 'outside'.

However, the house tables go one stage further by 'baptizing' these norms of a 'middle way'.[429] 'In the Lord' it is seemly to act in this way (Col.3.18): just as husbands are subordinate to the Lord, so should wives be to husbands, and husbands should love their wives as Christ loved the church (Eph.5.22-25). In this way this model of the relationship between the sexes, which was certainly not invented by Christians, is provided with a christological interpretation and thus divine authority. Only a heretic can now contradict it.

I Peter was written at about the same time as the Pastoral Epistles. Here too it is said that wives are to be subject to their husbands and husbands are to show their wives due honour (I Peter 3.1-7). There is as much said against the external adornment of women as there is in I Timothy. A new motive emerges. Women are to seek to win over their pagan husbands who are not obedient to the word of God and are to do this without words, i.e. through silence and subservience. If they succeed, a pagan ideal of virtue becomes the occasion for pagans to be converted to the Christian faith.

Paul was still concerned with peace in the communities (I Cor.14.33); a generation later order is conjured up. Paul could further correct (I Cor.11.11f.) what he said about the husband who is the head of the wife and the wife as being secondary in terms of creation (vv.3,7,8,9); a generation later there is no longer any correction; indeed what Paul corrected becomes a generally binding criterion. For women to be active in public inside and outside the Christian community is regarded by Christians as shameful. Thus all former activities through which women were of service in mission and building up the community were no longer available, indeed forbidden, to them. Only a few decades later it was possible to forget all these services on the part of women and to suppress them. In the name of Paul and with a false appeal to his authority this development was given biblical and christological support: just as Christ is the head of the husband, so is the husband the head of the wife: the exclusive responsibility of Eve for the fall proves the ethical inferiority of the female sex and the need for male supervision.

The Pastoral Epistles are evidence of the last stage of the development indicated in the New Testament. The charismatic beginnings had become history, and this was shown not least in the loss of prophecy.[430] The power of the prophetic word was replaced by structures of order, which sought to clear up the areas of conflict which had newly arisen: first Jews and Gentiles introduced different traditions, and thus customs and ordinances, into the Christian community, which retained their normative force by maintaining the social bond within the family. So it had to be decided which ordinances had the priority. Such ordinances always applied specially to the wives, tied to children and house, and so the conflicts were usually resolved to their disadvantage. To the degree to which 'a general morality of practical use in everyday life'[431] became established, they were again relegated to the ordering of the household. The life-style of discipleship had given way to a general humanistic sense of virtue. Thus a conservative adaptation to the world came about 'in which the church began to settle down and from which it derived the possibilities for its existence'.[432]

Secondly, conflicts increasingly developed between Christians of higher and lower status, between the rich and the poor. From the renunciation of possessions by the Jesus group, the model of life-style had moved through sharing and the giving of alms by the rich to pride in the prestige that the rich brought to the community. Luke, who wrote his work about thirty years after Paul, already puts stress on the rich, including the rich women from well-to-do circles, in order to lend splendour to the gospel.[433] With this emphasis on rich and well-to-do members of the community the Christians were responding to the criticism made by the pagans, which has already been mentioned,[434] of this new religion for the simple, the lowly, slaves and women. The Christians defended themselves by hastily adapting to the usual norms of behaviour: they sent their wives back home, asked them to keep quiet in public and made them bear children. 'A sober, upright and godly life in this world' (Titus 2.12) and circumstances which make possible a 'quiet and peaceable life, godly and respectful in every way' (I Tim. 2.2) now make it possible for Christian existence to have new characteristics. 'Being a Christian is expressed in a way which brings it close to "reasonable" and exemplary bourgeois behaviour. One may compare the frequency of such key words as modesty, honesty, piety, sound teaching, good conscience, and the catalogues of duties, virtues and vices.'[435] As house and family formed the social basis of the communities, the ascetical life-style was an alternative for those 'with gifts'. The new problem proved to be bringing marriage and family duties and the cares associated with them into accord with the gospel. The consequence of sharing tasks, giving women the family and men the ministry, was a further step in the name of order which led to the origin of paid ministers and replaced personal charisma with the grace of the ministry. In the hierarchy of ministries women are at best at the lowest level. Thus the not unjustified impression could arise that 'the church guaranteed the return of ancient Roman conditions – as promised by Augustus – especially the ordering of the household',[436] and thus served the interests of Roman conservatism.

Thirdly, and here we return to the first part of this chapter, the Gnosticism which brought hordes of Christians under its spell provoked rigid repudiation and reinforced the call for a fixed order, for 'sound' doctrine in opposition to 'sick heresy', for clearly defined functions of ministry and for women in the community who zealously brought children into the world for the continuance of Christianity. The statement from I Timothy that women are saved by bearing children (2.15) must have sounded abhorrent to Gnostic ears since the Gnostics abstained from sex and the production of descendants so as not always to imprison new light in matter. Therefore for them sexuality and eroticism are works of the wicked demiurge. The anti-Gnostic campaigns of the orthodox Christians therefore once again reinforced the direction of women to the household and to motherhood. Even more, it was only against the background of Gnostic sexual asceticism and hostility to children that the association of salvation with bearing children could have any comprehensible significance, if one keeps in mind the degree to which I Tim. 2.15 is a slap in the face to all the intentions of the Jesus movement.

Social dialectic

It is impossible to decide where Gnosticism originated, whether in pagan, Jewish or Christian circles. Even the Christian Gnostics differ widely in their degree of their proximity to the teaching and practice of the early church.[437] Evidently there was a Christian Gnosticism which was so closely bound up with the orthodox communities that the heresy hunters, e.g. the church father Irenaeus, complained that it was impossible to tell it apart.[438] Moreover Gnostics were active in church ministries, like Florinus as presbyter in the community in Rome, and Peter as presbyter and leader of a monastery near Hebron.[439] Furthermore, given such a connection it goes without saying that Gnostics were also members of orthodox communities. In addition there were separate Christian Gnostic communities in loose contact with church tradition[440] and Christian Gnostics who were excluded from the orthodox community and consequently formed their own communities. Like any attack on heresy, the polemic against the Gnostics also displays typical stages[441] and typical events: the isolation of the heretics could lead to an emigration from orthodox communities but also to a return into them.[442]

The Gnostics closely associated with the orthodox communities represented an extremely critical potential force over against the development indicated in connection with the Pastoral Epistles. The tractate 'The Interpretation of Gnosis' from the middle of the second century can be regarded as a Gnostic community order based on the Pauline model of personal charisma and so going against the adaptation of the early church to secular principles of order. Although the Pastoral Epistles also refer to the apostle, they no longer have anything in common with his idea of the community as a spiritual organism.[443] By contrast the Gnostics make the sharpest criticism of the ordering of the hierarchy of ministries, with or without reference to Paul: 'And there shall be others of those who are outside our number who make themselves bishop and also deacons, as if they have received their authority from God. They bend themselves under the judgment of the leaders. Those people are dry canals.'[444] The Gnostic can only see the conception that grace is communicated through a ministry and only through this – as the 'grace of the ministry' – as a tie to externals which belongs to the sphere of the archons hostile to God and goes against the Spirit. The same is true of an understanding of the church according to which membership of the church community is what determines salvation. The Gnostic understood the church to be an 'unworldly' community, the community of the pneumatics with the heavenly redeemer from the world of the pleroma. In the face of this, the earthly representation and organization of the church are unimportant, or important only for those who have not attained to true knowledge.[445] Taking their conviction to a logical conclusion the Gnostics also passed judgment on the church's sacraments: for the Gnostic, the elements of the sacraments, water, wine, bread, are matter in which no saving action can dwell,[446] certainly not in and of itself (*ex opere operato*); if this is at all possible it is possible only as the image of a spiritual reality to which gnosis alone provides access.[447]

One of the further charges of the Gnostics was that the church Christians could not and would not abstain from desire. One had to bid farewell to the world if one was not to be caught up in the power of the demiurge and his archons. However, this tendency towards the 'unworldly', bound up with the conception that this world was created by an evil hybrid, half light and half darkness,[448] is common to all Gnostics of various shades. By contrast, the church Christians are rooted in the world and lost to higher knowledge. They obey the law, not the Spirit. Through marriage and begetting children they continually imprison new divine light, instead of starving out the world.[449] In the course of anti-Gnostic polemic the church father Origen reports that on their return into the bosom of the church, ascetical heretics were even required to give up their ascetical life-style.[450] This sheds yet more light on the statement in I Timothy that women will be saved by bearing children. Moreover the criticism of the lack of continence on the part of orthodox Christians can also be associated with criticisms of 'serving mammon'.[451]

To all this the Gnostics opposed a pneumatic attitude. Unlike the church Christians they did not develop doctrinal traditions. Salvation for the Gnostic is a completely transcendent fact and can only be grasped spiritually. More than the church Christians, they are well up in the holy scriptures:[452] they practise exegesis, especially exegesis of Paul. Prophecies, discourses produced by the Spirit, understanding and preaching are numbered among the charismata,[453] as they were still in the time of Paul. Those Gnostics who live and work within the orthodox communities concede a certain justification for the existence of the church Christians in their imprisonment in externals. They have not got as far as the true Gnostics – yet? Where the church Christians do not want to understand themselves as being on the way but set their way of believing over against the Gnostics as the true way, they must appear to the Gnostics to be blind and therefore suffer their criticism.[454] From all this, and not least from the appeal of the Gnostics to Paul and his charismatic model of the community, it

becomes clear that women in Gnostic circles and communities
have, or regain, a role similar to that which we know from the
time of the letters of Paul. On this one point we must also agree
with Elaine Pagels' book.[455]

Over-hasty enthusiasm on behalf of the Gnostics is, however,
soon damped down when we see once again the conditions with
which the high estimation and collaboration of women in Gnostic
circles are associated: negation of the world, contempt for the
body, asceticism and the sense of being an élite. As a result of
these motives there is a link with the Jesus tradition, but not with
the intermediary period of the transition to the formation of
communities. This phase previously proved the most favourable
for women, though at the same time it marked the beginning of
developments which the Gnostics opposed – with a variety of
motivations.

Which came first? The Gnostic heresy, to which the church
Christians responded with principles of order? Or adaptation to
the standards of the world for the sake of a good reputation,
to which the heretics responded by hearking back to the old
charismatic tradition? Were all these developments 'necessary'
and thus unavoidable, or the result of guilt and failure? Feminists
argue for the guilt of the patriarchy which, even through Jesus
Christ, ultimately did not want power to be taken out of its
hands.[456] Men among the exegetes argue for a sociological principle: only a usable everyday ethic with the function of social
integration can guarantee continuity in history. Exodus and
contempt for the world do not, in the long run, help in that
direction.[457]

Both arguments are valid; to hold one against the other and
thus interpret all social conditioning as personal guilt or to deny
any guilt by referring to social conditioning would be wrong. The
battle between the sexes is always also a power struggle. In the
tradition of discipleship there was nothing to be gained because
Jesus and his followers had forsaken everything. Power and status
were explicitly rejected. In the later community the first disputes
arose over the variety of gifts. When Paul wants to restore the
balance by saying that the foot has just as much significance as
the head in the organism as a whole (I Cor.12.12), the head – the
function of leadership – is then regarded, as it is today, more in

terms of humble service. Where there are functions, ministries, public activity to gain, the battle begins, including that between men and women. As Paul speaks out so much about the quest for fame (e.g. I Cor.1.18ff.), one can infer a similar failing in his situation. Here it is a matter of power, struggle and – guilt. And the best weapon in the battle against the power of women has been at all times the bond between the woman and her children. Men have to decide to be responsible towards their children (and they often avoid that responsibility); women, however, are directly given into their children's hands if they do not want to sin by helpless creatures.

Human beings are always caught between the freedom to act from conscious motives and the bond to social structures which seem to lead a life of their own and which subject them.[458] Without the formation of communities and the developments connected with that the Jesus group would have been submerged in history as a somewhat marginal phenomenon. Because the Christians developed fixed social stuctures they could survive, but this was at the price of changes which had little in common with the conditions in which their 'founder' lived. The conflicts which emerge are typical: how does one resolve ethical differences, cases between poor and rich, the conflict between serving the gospel and duties to the family, the question of mixed marriages? Outside an exodus model, how can it be decided who really believes and who joins the Christian community for other, perhaps not very spiritual reasons? And if the Christians thought that they had to get a good reputation by adapting themselvs to secular ordinances, that is an understandable human reaction, for how long can one sustain the pressure of contempt and derogatory comments? If today a professional woman attempts to avoid prejudice by more than perfect organization of her household, the prejudice that in her position she could not but neglect her family, the underlying reason is a need comparable to that of Christians of the third generation: one has to be acknowledged and treasured among the children of men. From this perspective in the development of this period there is also a 'necessity', in the sense of unavoidable social pressures.

Because both sides are only human, it is hard to say which came first, the adaptation of Christians to the world or the denial of the world by heretics with all its aspects, including the positive ones. The effect is reciprocal, and different forces are in conflict in it: critical detachment, guilt, conflicts about which no one can do anything, human weakness, radicalism and renunciation, adaptation to the conditions of this world and the honest concern to lead a respectable life. Certainly orthodoxy and heresy are in conflict, but they condition each other and finally cannot get on without each other. Any heresy offers a legitimate criticism, even if it goes over the top, and any orthodoxy has good reasons for dissociating itself. Conversely, the rise of heretical groups is always a sign that orthodoxy has become heretical. The Christians of the church had transgressed against the pneumatic principle of the baptismal formula in Gal.3.28, which would have been tolerable a generation before under the conditions of orthodoxy; however, the Gnostics put this principle into practice at the cost of an ascetical retreat into élitism and imprisonment in increasingly deviant 'theologies'.

Thus the history of the New Testament canon can be taken as a lesson: it shows the truth as well as the guilt and the conflicts which are to be found in social systems. It can open our eyes more clearly to the distinction of these three levels, protect us from over-hasty judgments and illusions, help us to make decisions and offer us some eschatological constraints.

Moreover an accurate reading of the texts shows how non-Christian ideals of virtue were taken over and Christianized, while at the same time ascetical motivation retreated into the background. So asceticism and hostility do not necessarily go together, as a commonplace prejudice would have it. Rather, women seem to lose any other esteem where they are valued because of their sexuality: they are tied to the ordering of the house, put under the control of their husbands and used to ensure the procreation of the next generation. Again and again it is eros and the social reponsibility for children which keep women from tasks which they have in common with men, as a result of a reference to their 'natural duties'. The unprecedented stereotyping with which this theme is repeated through history puts the early history of Christian women in a wider context. The systematic questions which a critical examination of feminist theology cannot pass over will be the subject of another volume.

The Fire of the Spirit

1. So what – the reader of this book might ultimately ask – has a look at the history of Christian beginnings brought us other than confusion? On closer inspection current feminist judgments have proved untenable, because they go against the facts. Moreover, statements in the ancient texts which must be offensive to any feminist interest become understandable once we set them in the conditions of their time. The brief span of a few decades produces so many different estimations of women and the shared life of the sexes that all too many interests can refer to it: all models seem in some way justified and authorized, and the question of how much of them is binding remains unanswered in a haze of uncertainty.

So is it a mere matter of taste whether wives are subject to their husbands or found house communities and carry on missions? Whether they lead ascetic lives or bear a large number of children to prove to the Gnostics and their demiurge god what true Christian faith really is? Whether their martyrdom glorifies orthodoxy or is evidence of heresy?

If we begin from the fact that all these women had good intentions on the basis of which they made their decisions – when they had any possibility of making a decision – we must also concede that it was with the best will in the world that the men directed the women to the hearth or that it was with equal good will that for a while they allowed them greater privileges than usual. So if it were no more than a matter of taste and of subjective good will, we would remain detached onlookers who let history pass in front of them like a film, being impressed a little here and there, and then quickly returning to everyday reality.

This randomness does not lead to convictions nor is it a motive for action. That is evident at the latest in extreme cases: where you take a stand for what impels you, where you take a stand in extreme cases, even through martyrdom, your motivation must be presumed to be deeper. So what is the motivation towards action and resistance? What comprises that which is specifically Christian? What makes up Christian faith in the sense of that claim on reality which cannot be relativized through history?

2. Those looking for an answer can ask questions in two directions: first they can reconstruct history so as to give the most accurate answer possible to what actually happened at that time. This produces a picture of a time and its circumstances as a closed system, as apparently closed documentation. However, we cannot avoid the simple fact that in that case we always stand over against a picture created and framed in this way as those who are making a judgment, and we catch ourselves looking for criteria for assessing what has happened. Does it satisfy the claim to truth and the ethical demands which arise out of it? Should things have been as they were? Why are we agitated, for example, that there used to be slavery? Why do we take offence when in the Pastoral Epistles the bearing of children is said to be the way in which women achieve salvation? Or why are men not indifferent when they learn that women were active in preaching and carried on mission? When they are made to realize that the later model of subordination was not valid from the beginning?

It is not history which puts and answers the question what is true, correct or false, but the interest of a particular time which selects from history what it regards as being true, correct or false. This interest forms chains of motives which as a result of their context give the impression of being a closed system. History is a store room for materials of all kinds; no one hinders access to it, and whatever people want, they can find there.

This again poses the question how far what is true and correct can be freed from the whim of subjective estimation – women hold this to be correct and men hold that to be correct – in order for it to become a valid generalization. The stalemate between the historical object-ideal and the interest-orientated subject-ideal can produce a second possibility for the reconstruction of history. For the problem of both the difference of interests and the difference between interest and reality is not just ours: Christians, men and women, have from the start faced the question how the conviction of faith and the ordering of life can be expressed in binding statements. That means for us that statements about faith or ethics, in other words, about what is true or right, may only be regarded as binding (and that means set above the changing forces of history) if they themselves can be shown to be a living demand in the history to which we refer as Christians. The quest for the difference between what things are and what they should be, the contrast between the reality of the time and the truth-claim of the time, brings us close to the answer to the question of valid criteria. It is not the pluriform realities of history, or interests which are read in to that history, which stand at the focal point of this consideration, but human beings who know themselves to be open to claims and look for the realization of these claims.

That alone allows us to make valid comparisons: do our convictions and ethical claims correspond to those of the people who shaped the beginnings of Christianity? Do the conditions which then favoured or got in the way of the realization of these claims correspond to our present conditions? In this model both interest and historical facts in history are thus related and therefore do not fall apart for the contemporary observer of history.

But even in the texts of the New Testament itself, these considerations lead to useful distinctions. Statements which put men and women on the same level and statements which postulate a relationship of superiority or subordination at first sight emerge with the same timeless claim. But if one relates them to praxis they prove to have differing worth. Some begin from the praxis of Jesus and contrast it with the current behaviour of men and women (then as now); others begin from this current practice and contrast it with behaviour which only began in the second generation, though with reference to Jesus. Furthermore, some sentences are formulated in the negative: they stress the current difference in status, which was felt to be normal, between men and women, and leave the consequences of that to the historical possibilities at a particular time; other statements are put in the positive: they establish what a woman has to do and what she has not to do; they legitimate what is current and 'normal' and thus succumb to the normative power of the factual. Certainly not everything that is opposed to what actually happens is intrinsically

Christian; but it does make a significant difference whether a statement relativizes the factual and thus opens up possibilities for living or whether it keeps to the factual and thus prevents developments; whether a statement in the context of the preaching of the kingdom of God attracts a new reality or whether a statement in the context of the pragmatic baptizes the old reality.

3. The history of Christianity begins with the confession of the praxis of Jesus, which is opposed to the dominant life-style of his Jewish environment. Jesus himself understands it as the praxis of the kingdom of God, in which in principle the difference between the sexes has no place. Neither Jewish nor Hellenistic practice in relations between the sexes can be used to explain the derivation of the practice of Jesus. Here we see, rather, a claim against existing social practice made – like the other claims of the kingdom of God – under the conditions of what was then possible. Evidently what was possible at that time was to leave society: to be without possessions, without a home, without a spouse. Here we should therefore draw a distinction between the claim in principle and its realization in given circumstances. The criterion is not what was possible, nor are the claims the demand to give up possessions, home or spouse; so that is not a praxis which can be directly taken over, because it only reflects the claim through what is possible at any time. Thus where there is an attempt to imitate praxis as such in later history or to take it up again regardless, the difference between claim and reality has already been lost.

That is already evident at the next historical stage. After the death of Jesus and in the light of the confession of the resurrection, the community reflected on the nature of the Christian claim and by thus keeping the claim separate from praxis governed by the conditions of what was possible, succeeded in producing new forms of Christian life. There was also the opposite attempt, namely to argue from the practice of Jesus, who did not go outside the Jewish sphere, that all Gentiles who confessed the risen Christ had first to become Jews. In this approach the difference indicated above got lost. But the approach did not become established: the claim was recognized and expressed in the formulation of the baptismal formula of Gal.3.28, that there is 'neither Jew nor Greek, slave nor free, male nor female'. This statement mentions the claim and at the same time detaches it from practice, so that it can and must again be asked how the claim can be translated into new praxis under the new conditions of proclamation after Easter, community formation and mission, which have changed in comparison with the first beginnings.

The way taken by the first communities is therefore fundamentally different from the way of Jesus and yet follows the same claim. Under the conditions of settled life women now have even more possibilities for their active Christian life and preaching than was the case in the time of Jesus. An essential reason for this is to be found in the fact that now asceticism, and thus the renunciation of family and children, has been abandoned. It can be concluded from this that the claim to the equality and equal status of women in the kingdom of God cannot be realized solely in connection with asceticism. Conditions can change; but the important thing is always for ways to be found to realize a fundamental claim which has existed since the praxis of Jesus.

4. It is hard work to maintain the tension between claim and practice, and it is threatened at all times. Claims can become ideology when they do violence to reality, or they can evade the demands of reality; claims can also, however, get lost and become identified with prevailing practice. History is full of both these variants of the attempt to get free of the burden of the awareness of this difference and thus spare oneself the never-ending battle of realizing the claim. The tendency of the Christian communities at the end of the first and beginning of the second century was to obscure and to forget what should be, on the basis of the confession, in favour of what was superficially possible. This development led not least to the rise of heretical groups who justifiably, albeit one-sidedly, accorded a central place to what had originally been formulated as a claim: that here was neither man nor woman.

If we begin from the fact that the baptismal formula of Gal.3.28 was represented as something specifically Christian already by the Jesus group – and that seems to me to be indubitable – then we can consider whether important motives of the gospel did not pass over to heretical groups. As far as the claim of the abolition of the hierarchy of man and woman is concerned, however, to begin with this emigration did even more damage, because the confusion with conceptions which in fact have nothing to do with the Christian confession only strengthened the rejection from the orthodox side. At all events it is evident that demands which are not realized in praxis look for a new context: if the baptismal formula of Gal.3.28 were not a criterion of what is Christian and thus not permanently valid, it could have been given up, and could hardly have led to the rise of and motivation for new groups.

Charisma is constantly mentioned in connection with the beginnings of Christianity. There were not only times of awakening but also above all times in which claim and praxis were particularly clear as a result of the way in which they were distinguished. Charismatic periods give room and space for development to the Spirit as a supra-historical principle in historical practices. But charismatic times are characterized specifically by fulfilling to a large degree the maxim of Gal.3.28. According to Christian faith the claim and its realization will only coincide in the eschaton; nevertheless, the degree of the approximation of the two in history is no small matter, even if none of this could be maintained in the long run. And we must note that where praxis contains the claim or comes near to it, the question of women is not explicitly raised; there was no need for a 'feminist theology' either in the Jesus tradition or in the first communities. And where the role of women does become a question, namely in the late texts of the New Testament, praxis was already at a considerable remove from the claim: 'feminist theology' first takes shape in the form of an 'anti-feminist theology' with the attempt to diminish the doubly laborious dissociation from what is 'normal' in times of persecution and therefore to go against the heretical groups all the more clearly. What was originally an extremely orthodox statement, 'But it shall not be so among you...' (Mark 10.43), now became a principle of those who had left 'normal' community life: either outside to the heretics or within it to recognized, but separate, outsider groups such as we find throughout church history: orders, and reform and revival movements. Emigration of both kinds also threatens the church in the present day.

5. Against this background the perspective of questions and answers is reversed. The usual feminist history rummages through history and asks when and where women were oppressed, when and where they were accorded possibilities for development. Such

interest gives legitimation, and precisely in so doing does not correspond to the beginnings, or by contrast is very reduced in comparison with them. For if I begin from the fact that the practice of Jesus is authentically reflected in the baptismal formula of Gal.3.28, then women do not need legitimation from history, but the praxis of the church has to be accountable in the light of this criterion. It is the same with dealings with the poor, the oppressed and the alien, and today more than ever that is the criterion by which the practice of the church is measured; and the same thing goes for the position of women in the community. What sort of a role they do have in the group of those who are motivated by Christian faith is one of the central criteria for the Christian character of the church. Are they oppressed? Marginalized? Tolerated? Given alms? Compelled to legitimate themselves? The beginnings show that all that should not be necessary. They do not have to be asked what claims they make and on what these claims are based; they themselves are the living question to the church as to how far its practices, then and now, match up to the claim of Jesus.

Moreover the history which the canon of the New Testament records is not just a history of successful praxis: it delineates both the claim and its betrayal equally. That has also led to the development of a criticism of the canon and the working out of the canon in the canon in order to gain a criterion for individual texts, because evidently not all of them correspond in a comprehensive sense to what Christian faith holds to be true and requires. In this sense one can confidently put the question of the position of women in the church beside that of the canon in the canon. So it is not a matter of asking men to make more room for women; it is a matter of showing men with good reasons and with reference to the practice of Jesus and the community's confession of faith the criterion for how they are to behave towards women if they want to be Christians. A church which goes by the model of the Pastoral Epistles and does not see that the praxis evidenced in these letters has already moved a long way from the canon in the canon which women also represent has also removed itself from the claim of Jesus and makes itself guilty of both the internal and external emigration of its members.

It makes good sense for the canon not just to retain the truths and claims and to limit itself to writing down what should be done. The canon shows the struggle going on and the danger of forgetting, and in so doing it shows the task which has to be faced, then and now. It is that which can be learned from what is at first the confusing multiplicity of history. The interest of women is not an arbitrary one. It can refer to the claims made at the beginning and in that light pass judgment on the sheer 'anything is possible' of historical circumstances and events. By recognizing the variability of praxis but refusing to give up the claim women guard the fire of the Spirit which only generations that had become narrow-minded and anxious could confuse with the fire on the hearth at home.

Notes

1. E.G.Davis, *The First Sex*, Dent 1973, Penguin Books 1982.
2. Ibid., 35.
3. Ibid.
4. M.Hauke, *Die Problematik um das Frauenpriestertum vor dem Hintergrund der Schöpfungs- und Erlösungsordnung*, (dissertation) 1982.
5. Ibid., 178f.
6. Cf. S.Lehr, *Antisemitismus – Religiöse Motive im sozialen Vorurteil*, 1974; T.W.Adorno, *Studien zum autoritären Charakter*, [4]1982.
7. T.Moser, *Gottesvergiftung*, 1978.
8. T.W.Adorno, 'Zur Bekämpfung des Antisemitismus heute', in *Vorurteil*, Wege der Forschung, ed.A.Karsten, 1978, 222ff.,226.
9. Ibid,, 243.
10. M.Daly, *Gyn/ecology*, Beacon Press, Boston, and The Women's Press 1979, 23.
11. G.Schwarz, *Was Jesus wirklich sagte*, 1971, 65-6.
12. Cf. L.Schottroff, 'Maria Magdalena und die Frauen am Grabe Jesu', *Evangelische Theologie* 42.1, 1982, 3ff., 10f.; against, J.Blank, 'Frauen in den Jesusüberlieferungen', in *Die Frau im Urchristentum*, ed. G.Dautzenberg et al., 1983, 9ff., 53.
13. E.Pagels, *The Gnostic Gospels* (1980), Penguin Books 1982, 80f.
14. I.Illich, *Gender*, Marion Boyars 1983, 178.
15. Ibid.
16. For the concept of the horizon of motivation see H.Gehrke, *Theologie im Gesamtraum des Wirklichen*, 1981, 33ff.; Gehrke's work is 'an attempt to depict in outline Erich Heintel's theological system based on fundamental philosophy'.
17. M.Buber, 'Über das Erzieherische' (1919), in *Werke* I, 1962, 795f.
18. H.Gunkel, *Genesis* (1901), [8]1969, 16.
19. Ibid.
20. Ibid., 17.
21. Ibid., 22.
22. This kind of fiction, known as pseudepigraphy, should not be judged by present-day criteria of historical honesty. Pseudonymous writing was widespread in antiquity. The author of a work wanted to give status to or stress what he wrote by appealing in this way to an acknowledged authority. He did so in the subjective conviction that he had the closest association with the spirit of this authority, in the case of the Pastoral Epistles that of the apostle. The author wanted to write as Paul would have written. See 134f. below.
23. E.Kautzsch (ed.), *Textbibel des Alten und Neuen Testaments*, 1899, 151.
24. Sirach 25.24.

25. Apocalypse of Moses 7. This is extant in Greek and Armenian versions and goes back to a Hebrew original; it has a marked ascetical tendency.

26. Apocalypse of Moses 9. The text of the Apocalypse and that of the Life of Adam and Eve are printed in parallel in James H.Charlesworth (ed.), *Old Testament Pseudepigrapha* 2, Darton, Longman and Todd 1985, 249-95; translation by M.D.Johnson, here 271.

27. Ibid., 10: 273.

28. Ibid., 11: 274.

29. Ibid., 32: 287.

30. The Life of Adam and Eve 3: 258. This work also goes back to an original written in Hebrew and like the Apocalypse of Moses was later subjected to a Christian revision.

31. Life of Adam and Eve 10: 260.

32. Ibid., 18: 264.

33. Tertullian, *On the Apparel of Women* I.1.

34. IV Ezra has come down in many translations and was also included in the Vulgate. It goes back to a Hebrew original. It was very popular among Christians. This work is the genuine expression of a pessimistic apocalyptic understanding of existence; it was written after the destruction of Jerusalem in 70 but it dates the conversations and visions of Ezra back to the time of the destruction of Jerusalem in 587 BC. Historical crises were an occasion for asking about the meaning and future of creation. Text in Charlesworth, *Old Testament Apocrypha* 1, 1983, translation B.M.Metzger.

35. IV Ezra 3.16,7: 528. God is speaking to Ezra through the angel Uriel.

36. IV Ezra 3.21: 529; cf.v.26.

37. IV Ezra 7.11: 537.

38. IV Ezra 7.18: 541.

39. As the Syrian Apocalypse of Baruch seems to be dependent on IV Ezra, its date of origin is to be assumed to be the beginning of the second century. English text in Charlesworth, *Old Testament Apocrypha* 1, (= II Baruch) translation by A.J.F.Klijn.

40. II Baruch 17.2,3: 627.

41. II Baruch 54.15; cf.23.4: 640 cf. 629.

42. II Baruch 54.19: 640; on the one hand the texts mentioned contain the idea that Adam's sin cast the world into sin and death, and that all human beings are now bound up with his fate. On the other hand the individual responsibility of human beings is also made a theme. Both thoughts stand side by side without any connection between them.

43. II Baruch 56.5,6: 641.

44. The theory that Paul is referring back to elements of apocalyptic tradition with his Adam-Christ typology can be found above all in E.Käsemann, *Commentary on Romans*, 1980, 140ff.; O.Kuss, *Der Römerbrief*, 1, ²1963, 226ff.; H.Conzelmann. *I Corinthians*, Hermeneia, 1975, 284ff.; J.Weiss, *Der erste Brief an die Korinther*, MeyerK, reprint of ninth edition of 1910, 1970, 356.

45. I shall leave out of account the reinterpretation of the apocalyptic tradition which Paul makes through the christological context since my concern here is not with Pauline exegesis but with the underlying history of religions material.

Kuss rightly sees that for Paul the apocalyptic Adam tradition is subordinated to or set over against the apocalyptic Adam tradition, so Eve plays no part in it: only Adam can be an antitype for Jesus Christ (Kuss, 274 n.44). So it would be wrong to suppose here that Paul is particularly hostile to women.

Cf. the church father Irenaeus of Lyons, who puts the Eve-Mary typology in parallel to the Adam-Christ typology : 'The disobedience of the patriarch Adam entangled us all in the bonds of death. Therefore it was necessary and right that the fetters of death were broken by the obedience of the one who became man for us' (I, 31,1)... 'And as through the disobedience of a virgin mankind was caused to fall, fell and died, so through a virgin who hearkened to God's word, again ensouled with life, mankind received life' (I,3,33).

46. Augustine, *Enchiridion* (Handbook to Laurentius) 14.48. Cf. Augustine's *Letter to Boniface* 7-9.

47. Cyril of Jerusalem, *Baptismal Catechesis* 13.1-3.

48. John Chrysostom, *Homilies on Genesis* 18, cf.9.

49. *Homilies on Genesis* 14.

50. Thus e.g. in Wisdom 2.24; Ethiopian Enoch 69.6, etc.; cf.O.Kuss, *Römerbrief*, 269ff.

51. Cf. N.Füglister, 'Eva – ist die Frau an allem schuld?', in *Bibel heute* 79.3, 1984, 151.

52. Cf.P.Trible, *God and the Rhetoric of Sexuality*, Philadelphia ²1980, 113.

53. The hostility of feminists to method is either expressed directly, as e.g. by Mary Daly or Heide Göttner-Abendroth, or indirectly, through the call for an emotional, direct, imaginative, feminine relationship to the texts in the tradition, as e.g. by Elisabeth Moltmann-Wendel. As scientific methods have been the province of men for centuries and therefore have been governed by a different interest, feminists – and this is where the problem lies – identify them with male interest and reject anything that looks like method as being patriarchal. For the identification of method and interests cf. E.Schüssler-Fiorenza, 'Der Beitrag der Frau zur urchristlichen Bewegung', in *Traditionen der Befreiung*, ed. W.Schottroff and W.Stegemann, 2, 1980, 60ff.

54. Cf.K.Berger, *Exegese des Neuen Testaments. Neue Wege vom Text zur Auslegung*, 1977, 123ff.; W.Eichrodt, *Theology of the Old Testament* II, 1967, 402ff.: J.Sløk, 'Mythos und Mythologie', *RGG³*, IV, 1960, 1263f.

55. Sløk, op.cit., 1263.

56. Genesis 3 belongs to the Yahwistic stratum of tradition. The texts of the Old Testament have been woven together from different sources, and historical-critical exegesis attempts, for example, to distinguish, locate and describe these sources. The unknown figure behind the tradition has been called the Yahwist because of a distinctive characteristic: he uses the name Yahweh for God (at all events, this applies to Genesis). His literary works are coloured by a joy in the fertile land that has been won, sedentary life, and a monarchy with which great national hopes are associated for the people, which has a tendency towards apostasy from God.

57. Canaan is the pre-Israelite name for the coastal strip of Palestine and Syria, which is attested at an early date; this name was taken over by the Israelite tribes and was in use until the formation of the state. After that the land was known as Israel.

58. Cf. A.Alt (R.Bach), 'Kanaan–geschichtlich', *RGG³* III, 1959, (cols.1109ff.) 1110.

59. R.Graves, *The Greek Myths* 1, Penguin Books ²1960 (the Pelasgian creation myth), 27.

60. The prophetic criticism of the monarchy in Israel is shown in action in the appearance of prophets against particular kings (e.g. Samuel against Saul, Nathan

against David, Elijah against Ahab, to mention just a few). The prophet accompanies the king like a shadow.

61. Füglister, *Eva*, 151.

62. Cf. the argument by O.Kuss, which has a similar structure, though not a similar content (n.45 above).

63. Thus e.g. Simone de Beauvoir, Betty Friedan, Mary Daly, Heide Göttner-Abendroth.

64. Thus e.g. Elisabeth Moltmann-Wendel, Elisabeth Schüssler-Fiorenza, Luise Schottroff; Rosemary Ruether is very critical, though she has not given up looking for elements of humanity in Christian tradition. H.Pissarek Hudelist, 'Feministische Theologie – eine Herausforderung', *Zeitschrift für Katholische Theologie* 103, 1981, 289ff., gives an account of the various positions in feminism and feminist theology.

65. M.Daly, *Gyn/ecology*, 23f. etc.

66. M.Daly, *The Church and the Second Sex* (1968), ²1985, 106.

67. Ibid., 109.

68. Cf. S.Heine, 'Wissensvermittlung als Wissenschaftskritik', *Wiener Jahrbuch für Philosophie*, ed. E.Heintel/H.D.Klein, Vol.XVII, 1985, 59ff.; cf. also P.L.Berger and B.Berger, *Wir und die Gesellschaft*, (1972) 1976, 127ff.

69. Ibid., 19ff.

70. Cf. J.Scharfenberg, 'Martin Luther in psychohistorischer Sicht', in *Europa in der Krise der Neuzeit. Martin Luther: Wandel und Wirkung seines Bildes*, ed. S.Heine, 1986, 113ff.

71. Tertullian, *To his Wife*, II.9.

72. Tertullian, *On the Apparel of Women*, II, 13.

73. Tertullian, *To his Wife*, I,2.

74. Ibid.

75. At the time of Tertullian North Africa had on several occasions been affected by persecutions of Christians. There is reason to suppose that Tertullian also wrote the Acts of the martyrs Perpetua and Felicitas (the women were killed with other Christians under Severus in 199).

76. Tertullian, *To his Wife*, I,5.

77. Tertullian, *On the Apparel of Women*, II.13.

78. 'Gnostic' is the term applied to ascetic religious groups in late antiquity which were combated by the church as threatening and stubborn heretics, and were finally defeated. See Chapters 6 and 7 below, 106ff.

79. E.g. Celsus, against whom the church father Origen defended the Christian faith (second century): cf. *Celsus, Against the Christians*, ed. H.Chadwick, Cambridge University Press 1953. Cf.further the dialogue *Octavius* by Minucius Felix. Here the pagan Caecilius argues against the Christian Octavius (also second century). Augustine is one of those who reply to the criticism of the philosopher Porphyry (third century, cf. e.g. *City of God*, XIX, 23), and the church historian Eusebius replies to that of Hierocles. Cf. R.L.Wilken, *The Christians as the Romans Saw Them*, 1984.

80. Cf. the apt judgment by Werner Raith on Tertullian in *Das verlassene Imperium*, 1982, 145ff. However, Raith is anachronistic in trying to interpret Tertullian with concepts like 'attack on the system' (146). Tertullian's attitude is not the result of sociological analysis; his thought is not a 'criticism of the system'. F.W.Korff (in the Preface to the German edition of *Contra Celsum* edited by T.Keim, 1984) aptly describes Raith's tendency as a 'non-identifiable Marxism

of a green kind'. Nevertheless the book offers interesting and accurate insights, and is also amusing to read.

81. The critics were drawn from the circle of philosophers (especially the Stoics and Cynics), the priesthood and the politicians.

82. Augustine, *City of God* (IV.4).

83. Cf. Raith, *Das verlassene Imperium*, 67ff., 134ff.

84. Korff, *Contra Celsum*, 11.

85. Columella (first century), *On Agriculture* (Book 1, Preface, 6). Instead of devoting themselves to despicable immoralities like mathematics, music, oratory and law or demeaningly haggling over 'the splendour of office and the violence of command' and spending good money on them, people should practise agriculture, the 'only way of increasing one's possessions which is respectable and worthy of a free man'.

86. Raith, *Das verlassene Imperium*, 145.

87. It is possible to pass either a positive or a negative judgment on such a refusal. That also applies to the rise of Christians which is associated with it. Thus Korff, *Contra Celsum*, sees predominantly the losses in this development: an aggressive monotheism takes the place of a peace-loving natural religion, nature loses its soul, and man becomes presumptuous, without feeling for family and state: 'People went to the old religions (he means the pagan ones) with a good conscience clad in white and freshly washed; they greeted the gods standing and did not fall on their knees; now pale neurotic figures meet who tell one another of their sins' (15). Peter Brown, *The Making of Late Antiquity*, 1978, attempts a judgment in keeping with the time which does not see the last centuries of the Roman empire at any price as being a reflection of 'modern European crises'. He is concerned to 'note the specific details of the way in which life was maintained and survival ensured in what at that time was the by no means economically undeveloped environment of the pre-industrial Mediterranean world' (ibid.).

88. Tertullian, *On the Pallium* V.

89. Cf.n.87. One must remain aware of the danger of introducing one's own experiences and judgments into history. Raith is all too ready to draw direct parallels; by contrast Brown's dispassionate detachment, which seeks to allow history its due, suggests refraining from making any connections. However, on closer inspection Brown too seeks to establish a connection, but he does it in a different way from Raith; he wants to become one of the dead so as to raise them to life. Here we can see a typical feature: historical analyses always move between Scylla and Charybdis, between 'absorbing' the past, taking it into the present reality, and going into past reality, 'escaping' into past time. The former threatens the loss of past identity, the latter the loss of present identity. The solution to the problem lies in the power to maintain both conflicting tendencies in their dialectical tension.

90. Tertullian, *On the Soul*, XXX 4.

91. Cf.Tertullian, *On the Games, On Idolatry, On the Martyrs*.

92. Tertullian. *On the Adornment of Women*.

93. Tertullian, *To his Wife*.

94. Tertullian introduces his work *On Baptism* in the following words: 'A treatise on this matter will not be superfluous; instructing not only such as are just becoming formed, but those who, content with having simply believed, without full examination of the grounds of the traditions, carry in mind through ignorance an untried though probable faith.' On the dialectic of Aristotle he

writes: 'so far-fetched in its conjectures, so harsh in its arguments' (*The Prescription against Heretics* 7). Cf. Mary Daly: 'The acceptable/unexceptional circular reasonings of academics are caricatures of motion.' Mary Daly, too, calls for faith by rejecting any 'right re-search' as 'ritual', *Gyn/Ecology*, 23.

95. Daly, *The Church and the Second Sex*, 86, 87f.

96. Pagels, *The Gnostic Gospels*, 87f.

97. Tertullian. Like God, so too faith has 'foolishness and impossibility as its object' (*On Baptism* 2). This notion keeps recurring in Tertullian.

98. Pagels, *The Gnostic Gospels*, 87.

99. Clement of Alexandria, *Stromateis* II, 140.

100. Clement of Alexandria, *Stromateis* II, 140.

101. Clement of Alexandria, *Stromateis* II, 141. For flight in persecution cf. IV, 76,1ff.

102. H.Kanz, 'Anmerkungen zu Clemens' von Alexandrien Schrift "Der Erzieher" [*Paidagogos*] (I.4)', in *Klemens von Alexandrien. Ausgewählte Schriften zur Pädagogik*, ed. H.Kanz, 1966, 78.

103. Clement of Alexandria, *Paidagogos* I, 10.1-2; 11.1.

104. Clement of Alexandria, *Paidagogos* III, 49.3.

105. Clement of Alexandria, *Stromateis* IV, 59.3-4; 60.1.

106. Clement of Alexandria, *Stromateis* IV, 61.3.

107. Clement of Alexandria, *Stromateis* IV, 62.4.

108. Clement of Alexandria, *Paidagogos* III, 49.2.

109. Clement of Alexandria, *Paidagogos* III, 49.3-4.

110. Clement of Alexandria, *Paidagogos* III, 46.1.

111. Clement of Alexandria, *Stromateis* II, 140f.

112. This contrast indicates the basic tenor of the attitude of the two church fathers, but no contrast in a purist direction should be developed from it. In connection with marriage Tertullian also commends the subjection of wives to their husbands; and Clement can also argue for abstinence, e.g. in order to be able to beget children without lust and desire with a view to Christ. Tertullian, *On the Apparel of Women*, II, 13; Clement of Alexandria, *Stromateis* III, 58.2.

113. See above, 27.

114. Ernst Troeltsch, for example, gave a very good account of the dialectical relationship between 'individual fact' and the 'overall context' as a problem of historical method: 'Über historische und dogmatische Methode in der Theologie', *Gesammelte Schriften* II, ed. H.Baron (Vols.I-1V, 1912-25), 729ff. The individual fact gains and changes its significance in the light of the whole context and the whole context takes its form from the individual facts; not, however, as a simple sum but as a system. Cf. below the remarks on the motive-historical method (111f.).

115. There is also a dialectical connection between the historical 'object' and the present and interested subject. Historical research presupposes interest and will also constantly put this interest in question with sufficient insight into this dialectic. Thus again both the interest and consequently the object and the result of research change. There is a price to be paid for abandoning this dynamic: what follows is either the separation of the two sides into 'purely objective' (which is impossible) and 'purely subjective' (which has nothing to do with history) or a confusion arises which leads to hopeless perplexity, because the one side is exchanged for the other. As the feminist argument usually tends towards confusion or a one-sided stress on the subject side, the object side has to be

stressed, though with a reference to the danger that the dialectic may again be resolved in favour of the 'purely objective'.

116. To give an example, there is neither confirmation nor refutation in history for the following statement by the Austrian diocesan bishop Dr Kapellari. The Roman Catholic Church feels itself 'bound in the light of Jesus to reserve the priestly office for men' (in *Kathpress* (Vienna) *Informationsdienst* 34, 23 August 1985,1). But Jesus did not institute any priesthood. The only thing that emerges clearly from this is the interest at work. But history again does not contradict that clearly enough, because the interest of the bishop mentioned was not known to Jesus, in such a way that he could have given a clear answer to it.

117. All the feminist authors say that feminist theology uses a new, indeed a specific, feminist method. A 'gynocentric form of writing' is called for and practised instead of an androcentric one (Daly, *Gyn/ecology*). Cf. R.Ruether, *Sexism and God Talk*, 1983.

118. This term was coined by Simone de Beauvoir, who died in April 1986.

119. A.Schütz, *Das Problem der Relevanz*, ed.R.M.Zaner, 1982, 100ff.

120. Cf.e.g. R.Oerter, *Moderne Entwicklungspsychologie*, [10]1971, 215ff.

121. See n.16. Cf. E.Heintel, 'Gott ohne Eigenschaften', in *Gott ohne Eigenschaften*, ed. S.Heine and E.Heintel, Evangelischer Presseverband 1983, (9ff.) 23f.

122. Schütz, *Das Problem der Relevanz*, 113.

123. Ibid., 100.

124. Ibid., 113.

125. I deliberately speak of motivation being 'unclear' rather than 'unconscious'. Answering the question whether a person is acting consciously or unconsciously presupposes an intimate knowledge of the person which is possible at best in psychoanalytical praxis and not in everyday converse. That is all the more true of people who are separated from us by decades, if not centuries. Cf. Berger, *Exegese des Neuen Testaments*, 166; cf. n.70.

126. Ibid., 260.

127. In developmental psychology people talk of 'controlled experience of discrepancy' or the 'principle of incongruity' which acts as a motive. However, the deviation from the familiar must not be too great, as otherwise reactions of anxiety and refusal can be set off. Cf. F.E.Weinert et al. (eds.), *Pädagogische Psychologie*, Funk-kolleg 1,[5]1977, 125f.

128. Schütz, *Das Problem der Relevanz*, 106.

129. Ibid., 101

130. K.Mannheim, *Wissenssoziologie*, ed. K.M.Wolff, 1964, 251.

131. Ibid., 258.

132. K.Mannheim, *Ideology and Utopia*, Routledge 1954, 259.

133. Mannheim, *Wissenssoziologie*, 263.

134. Ibid., 287.

135. H.Albert, 'Wertfreiheit als methodisches Prinzip', in *Logik der Sozialwissenschaften*, ed. E.Topitsch, [8]1972, 190.

136. Mannheim, *Wissenssoziologie*, 270.

137. Ibid., 287.

138. Ibid.

139. See above 10f.

140. Bernadette Brooten is a Roman Catholic theologian who was born in the USA, spent a long time in the University of Tübingen and went on to teach there. At the moment she is researching into and teaching biblical studies as an Assistant

Professor at Harvard Divinity School. Elisabeth Schüssler-Fiorenza is also a Roman Catholic theologian; she was born in Germany and teaches New Testament at the Episcopal Divinity School in Cambridge, Massachusetts.

141. John Chrysostom, *Commentary on Romans*, Homily 32.

142. *Novum Testamentum Graece*, ed. E.Nestle and K.Aland, seventh revised impression of ²⁶1985.

143. A.von Harnack, 'Probabilia über die Adresse und den Verfasser des Hebräerbriefes', *ZNW* 1, 1900, 16ff.

144. The reason why the texts say less about women than about men is connected with the 'androcentric' textual tradition. E.Schüssler-Fiorenza keeps referring to this in *In Memory of Her. A Feminist Reconstruction of Christian Origins*, SCM Press and Crossroad Publishing Company 1983, 41ff.

145. Tertullian, *On Flight in Persecution* (12), PL 2,114ff., 116.

146. G.Dautzenberg et al (eds.), *Die Frau im Urchristentum*, Quaestiones disputatae 95, 1983.

147. See n.53.

148. *Die Frau im Urchristentum* (Preface), 5f.

149. M.Bussmann, 'Anliegen und Ansatz feministischer Theologie', in *Die Frau im Urchristentum*, (339ff.) 358.

150. The contribution from Ms Schüssler-Fiorenza was asked for by the editors of the Schnackenburg Festschrift but was then rejected for publication. That was in 1979. Thereupon the author published her article elsewhere in 1980 (cf. n.53). The *Festschrift* for Schnackenburg took three years more to appear. Since the dates of publication of the two books are confusing because of the gap that transpired, a short explanation seems necessary.

151. Ibid.

152. Cf. the much quoted 'evidence' for such practice in the journal of Amnesty International, Austrian section (A.Pühringer and R.Francan).

153. The literature on violence against women has meanwhile grown to a considerable degree. See particularly B.Kavemann and I.Lohstöter, *Väter als Täter*, 1984; S.Brownmiller, *Against our Will*, Simon and Schuster 1975.

154. Ivan Illich uses the concept of 'shadow work' in *Gender* (n.14), see esp. 45ff.

155. Cf. e.g. I.Rowhani-Ennemoser, *Kleine Diebinnen lässt man niemals laufen*, 1982.

156. See n.116.

157. Mannheim, *Wissenssoziologie*, 281.

158. Ibid., 271.

159. This 'hidden connection' is called dialectic in philosophy. Arno Anzenbacher gives a clear and simple definition of dialectic: 'One speaks of a dialectic situation when something can be understood only in terms of two opposed elements... Here these two elements are always related. One points to its opposite. Taken by itself, in other words without the other, each of these elements is one-sided, abstract, a partial aspect. The aspects have concrete significance only when they are transcended in the true whole, that is, in their result' (*Einführung in die Philosophie* 1981, 96).

160. Mannheim, *Wissenssoziologie*, 273.

161. Ibid., 269.

162. Ibid., 279.

163. Ibid., 273.

164. A.Schweitzer, *The Quest of the Historical Jesus (1910)*, A. and C. Black 1954[3], 4.

165. Ibid.

166. Ibid., 38.

167. K.Mannheim, *Wissenssoziologie*, 269f.

168. Above, 37ff.

169. A.Schütz, *Das Problem der Relevanz*, 130.

170. Cf. C.Benard and E.Schlaffer, *Die ganz gewöhnliche Gewalt in der Ehe*, 1978. A report on the ecumenical marriage of Frau Schlaffer appeared in the Viennese journal *Falter* 15, July/August 1985 under the title 'The Finest Day'.

171. Cf. C.Benard and E.Schlaffer, *Der Mann auf der Strasse*, 1980.

172. *Falter* 16, August 1985, 'Open Letter'.

173. Schweitzer, *Quest of the Historical Jesus*, 4.

174. Mannheim, *Wissenssoziologie*, 271.

175. Berger, *Exegese des Neuen Testaments*, 260.

176. I shall not list feminist positions because these can be found in many books which have appeared in the meantime, cf. n.64. I would, however, like to draw attention to the book by Barbara Sichtermann, *Weiblichkeit. Zur Politik des Privaten*, 1983, which in my view is noted too little on the 'market', not least because I share the view of the future that is put forward there in the preface.

177. H.Wolff, *Jesus der Mann. Die Gestalt Jesu in tiefenpsychologischer Sicht*, 1975.

178. Ibid., 59.

179. Ibid., 82.

180. Ibid., 25f.

181. Ibid., 19. Here Wolff bases her views on the anthropology of F.J.J.Buytendijk.

182. Whereas E.Moltmann-Wendel appeals to Hanna Wolff (see n.183, 13), Gerda Weiler offers a markedly critical view (*Der enteignete Mythos*, 1984).

183. E.Moltmann-Wendel, *The Women around Jesus*, SCM Press and Crossroad Publishing Company 1982, 71.

184. Ibid., 61ff., 70.

185. See n.144.

186. The following literature in particular underlies these sociological comments: E.Troeltsch, *The Social Teaching of the Christian Churches*, Lutterworth Press 1931; A.von Harnack, *The Mission and Expansion of Christianity in the First Three Centuries* (1906), reissued 1952; M.Hengel, *Die Zeloten*, 1961; E.A.Judge, *The Social Pattern of Christian Groups in the First Century*, Tyndale Press 1960; J.Jeremias, *Jerusalem in the Time of Jesus*, SCM Press and Fortress Press 1967; E.Lohse, *The New Testament Environment*, SCM Press and Abingdon Press 1976; J.G.Gager, *Kingdom and Community. The Social World of Early Christianity*, Prentice-Hall 1975; G.Theissen, *The First Followers of Jesus*, SCM Press 1978; id., *Studien zur Soziologie des Urchristentums*, WUNT 19,[2]1983; S.Safrai et al. (eds.), *The Jewish People in the First Century, Compendia Rerum Iudaicarum ad Novum Testamentum*, two vols, 1976; K.Thraede, 'Ärger mit der Freiheit', in *Freude in Christus werden*, ed. G.Scharffenorth and K.Thraede 1977, 31ff,; W.A.Meeks, *The Sociology of Primitive Christianity*, Fortress Press 1979; F.Belo, *A Materialist Reading of the Gospel of Mark*, Orbis Books 1981; M.Clevenot, *Materialist Approaches to the Bible*, Orbis Books 1982. Cf. also W.G.Kümmel's critical survey of the literature, 'Das Urchristentum. Zur Sozialgeschichte und Soziologie der Urkirche', *ThR* 50, 1985, 327ff.

187. Cf. the problem of method in the social sciences. On the one hand social reality is created and formed by the motivated action of subjects, and on the other reality has the character of massive objectivity on which subjects can break up.

188. Raith, *Das verlassene Imperium*, 119.

189. Theissen, *The First Followers of Jesus*, 34ff.

190. Cf.M.Hengel, *Die Zeloten*, 1961.

191. Josephus, *Jewish War*, VII, 320.

192. Ambrose, *Commentary on Luke*, 9.34-36.

193. The text is a slightly free for purposes of emphasis.

194. Theissen, *The First Followers of Jesus*, 17.

195. In Luke, however, a tendency towards idealization must be taken into account,

196. I have found no such reference in scholarly commentaries. E. Moltmann owes us an instance (*The Women around Jesus*, 134). If by theologian she means preacher I can back her up from my own experience.

197. L.Schottroff, 'Frauen in der Nachfolge Jesus in neutestamentlicher Zeit', in *Traditionen der Befreiung*, (91ff.) 107.

198. Blank, 'Frauen in der Jesusüberlieferung', in *Die Frau in Urchristentum*, (9ff.) 53.

199. Ibid., cf. K.H.Rengstorf, *Das Evangelium nach Lukas*, NTD 3, ⁹1962, 105.

200. Theissen, *The First Followers of Jesus*, 17.

201. E.Schüssler-Fiorenza, 'The Role of the Woman in the Primitive Christian Movement', *Concilium* 12, 1976, (3ff.) 4 (= 'Der Beitrag der Frau': though the English title of this article is given, it was published at a time when not all the issues of *Concilium*, including this one, were appearing in English).

202. That Jesus had physical brothers and sisters has meanwhile also been recognized by Roman Catholic exegetes out of historical honesty, R.Pesch, *Das Markusevangelium*, 1.Teil, Herder-Kommentar NT 1976, 322f.

203. Cf. below, 69f.

204. Cf. e.g. Theissen, *The First Followers of Jesus*, 14f.

205. Thus L.Schottroff (n.53), 101, in opposition to Theissen.

206. Cf. Belo, *A Materialist Reading of the Gospel of Mark*, 173f.

207. Cf.L.Schottroff, 'Frauen in der Nachfolge Jesu', 104f., 129 n.54.

208. Clement of Alexandria, *Stromateis* III, 53,3.

209. Shalom ben Chorin, *Bruder Jesus. Der Nazarener in jüdischer Sicht*, ⁶1983, 104.

210. Theissen, *The First Followers of Jesus*, 11.

211. E.Moltmann-Wendel, *The Women around Jesus*, 68, 70.

212. L.Schottroff, 'Die Frau', 104.

213. For the distinction between asceticism arising out of a tabu anxiety and asceticism for the sake of the kingdom of heaven cf. K.Niederwimmer, *Askese und Mysterium*, 1975, cf. e.g., 5, etc. Using psychoanalytical terminology the author speaks of repression asceticism and renunciation asceticism. In the sphere of theoretical conceptuality this distinction is possible and helpful, but where it is 'applied' to particular people in history (and the same also goes for those alive today), the difficulties already mentioned begin (see n.70). Niederwimmer does not take this methodological problem into account. He transfers the psychological interpretament in a linear way to the text. Moreover the term 'renunciation asceticism' does not indicate that such a renunciation is often used for a goal

which is given preference. The renunciation is only the other side of the 'delight' with which an ascetic pursues his or her goal.

214. S.Safrai, 'Religion in Everyday Life', in *The Jewish People in the First Century*, 2, (793ff.) 827.

215. Theissen, *The First Followers of Jesus*, 80.

216. Josephus, *Antiquities* XX, 9.2.

217. Cf. Plato, *Republic* 360c-361d.

218. Safrai, 'Religion in Everyday Life', 820.

219. Some exegetes dispute that Jesus understood himself as Messiah. Their view is that only after Easter did the Christian community transfer messianic conceptions to Jesus, not without changing them.

220. Tacitus, *Annals* 6.19.

221. L.Schottroff, 'Maria Magdalena und die Frauen am Grabe', *Evangelische Theologie* 42.1, 1982, (3ff.) 18f.

222. R.Bultmann, *The History of the Synoptic Tradition*, Blackwell and Harper & Row ²1968, 274.

223. Ibid.

224. R.Pesch, *Das Markusevangelium* 1, 508 n.16.

225. In the meanwhile this view of Paul has become a kind of commonplace within and outside the feminist 'camp'.

226. Cf. e.g. Mary Daly already in her initial phase, *The Church and the Second Sex*, 49f.

227. Cf. W.D.Thomas, 'The Place of Women in the Church at Philippi', *Expository Times* 83, 1972, 117ff.

228. Flavius Josephus, *Jewish War* II,19.

229 Ibid., II,20,2.

230. There is also mention of godfearers among the women in Acts 13.50, and of godfearers among the men in Acts 8.26.

231. It can be taken as proved that this passage is pre-Pauline traditional material. Cf. K.Stendahl, *The Bible and the Role of Women*, Fortress Press 1966; H.Thyen, '...nicht mehr männlich und weiblich...', in *Als Mann und Frau geschaffen*, ed. F.Crüsemann and H.Thyen, 1978. 107ff.; W.A.Meeks, 'The Image of the Androgyne', in *History of Religion* 13, 1973, 165ff.; etc.

232. This commonplace is variously derived from Thales or Plato, cf. Meeks, op.cit., 167 n.7.

233. Often handed down by rabbinic literature (Talmud) and in variants, cf. op.cit., 168 n.9.

234. Thus e.g. A.Oepke, *Der Brief des Paulus an die Galater*, THNT IX, ²1957, 90f.; cf. G.Dautzenberg, 'Zur Stellung der Frauen in den paulinishen Gemeinden', in *Die Frau in Urchristentum* (n.146), (182ff.) 216ff.

235. One should reflect on this before accusing women of aggressiveness, a lack of readiness to cooperate and a lack of will for reconciliation and dismissively refer to them as 'emancipated'. Clearly people tend to pay less attention to arguments than to vehement attacks.

236. For the exegesis of Phil.4.2-3 cf. W.Schenk, *Die Philipperbriefe des Paulus. Kommentar*, 1984. Schenk puts forward the theory that the two women were not in dispute but were accomplices in the dispute with parts of the community because as leaders of the communities they had opened up their house communities to false teachers (272). Such motives, limiting the function of women to leading house communities (though at least the interpretation would have to be put forward as one possibility among others) and the suspicion that

women would have had a ready ear for heretics, are among the characteristic signs of misogynistic polemic (cf. n.242). In view of the scanty textual material the reader is amazed what powerful wings polemic can lend to fantasy.

237. The text of Philippians is not a unity, so that it is not unnatural to divide it into several letters which were later formed into one composite one. Cf. Schenk, who distinguishes three letters: letter A – letter of thanks from Paul in prison for the gifts of money from the community; B – a letter from the apostle, now free again, brought by Epaphroditus; C – a warning letter which relates to false teachers in the community. This division, like so much else in an effort at reconstruction, is a hypothesis, though there are some things to be said for it. But there are also commentators who argue for the unity of the letter (e.g. E.Lohmeyer) or for dividing it into two. Whether 'fellow-prisoner' means that the two women were imprisoned in the same prison as Paul or separately cannot be determined, nor does it seem very important.

238. See above, 41f.

239. See above, 42ff.

240. Cf.G.Lohfink, 'Weibliche Diakone im Neuen Testament', in *Die Frau im Urchristentum*, (320ff.) 326.

241. The feminine 'deaconess' is only attested for the second century, ibid.

242. Cf. Käsemann, *Commentary on Romans*, 409.

243. Ibid., 411.

244. E.Schüssler-Fiorenza, 'Der Beitrag der Frau', 65f.

245. Käsemann, *Commentary on Romans*, 392.

246. G.Lohfink, 'Weibliche Diakone', in *Die Frau im Urchristentum*, 323: '...that the churches' ministry in the first decades was not yet grounded in the celebration of the eucharist. At first it was not yet interpreted as a sacral priestly ministry.'

247. Cf. K.Thraede, 'Ärger mit der Freiheit', 101f.,

248. Ibid., 77f.

249. Ibid., 80.

250. Cf. von Harnack, *Mission and Expansion*, 385f. There is also evidence of mixed marriages between Christian women and pagan priests (393f., 395).

251. Cf. ibid., 393f., etc.

252. Tertullian, *De Corona* 4.

253. Thus aptly H.Thyen, '...nicht mehr männlich', 160ff. Thyen rightly points out that the society of the Empire did not live in a 'pre-revolutionary situation'. Not taking seriously the conditions of 'this aeon', of this world, also amounts to a political praxis (167). Cf. Troeltsch, *The Social Teaching of the Christian Churches*, 79ff.

254. Cf. S.Heine, *Leibhafter Glaube*, 1976, 140f.

255. See above, 31.

256. Paul's ascetical attitude is often grounded solely on this imminent expectation; he is said to have expected the end of the world in his lifetime and therefore to have counselled against marriage and having children. That is an individualistic reduction. At most the imminent expectation may be introduced as one of Paul's reasons for not marrying, but it is an element that we can hardly grasp now: none of the expectations of the destruction of the world which have arisen in the course of two thousand years has so far been confirmed. The argument for imminent expectation as an individual problem for Paul is often used to dissociate the writer from an ascetical attitude. All the other motives of the apostle which I attempted to outline are much more closely connected with

our experience. Where people do not want to note these motives one can suppose a prejudice, as is usually the case with monocausal models.

257. An intermediate form evidently practised at the time of Paul is represented by the *syneisactai*, in Latin termed *virgines subintroductae*. In this model a man and woman live together for the sake of Christian fellowship, but without erotic sexual relationships. It is understandable that it was not easy to remain an ascetic in these circumstances. Paul's comments in I Cor. 7.36-37 can only be understood on these presuppositions.

258. Faith, too, is a social reality. Paul himself gives a good example of that in connection with the question whether a Christian may eat flesh which has been offered to idols, i.e. pagan gods. A Christian knows, says Paul, that there are no idols; 'for us' there is only one God (I Cor.8.4-6). So the Christian must not have any conscience about eating this flesh. That is one side, the side of personal faith. The other side is that where people believe in idols and practise this faith in a community, the idols get effective power (I Cor.10.28). The one is a recognition of the individual (in Paul's case understood in this context as an insight of faith); the other is the reality of a faith lived out in a society which is so strong that it can endanger the insight. Paul recognized the disastrous splitting of reality into individual and social (as we would say in contemporary terms) as a structural problem. His arguments apply in principle both to the Christian and the pagan community of faith. Cf. Heine, *Leibhafter Glaube*, 1976, 90ff.

259. Pagels, *The Gnostic Gospels*, 72.
260. Ibid.
261. Ibid., 73.
262. Ibid., 81.
263. Ibid., 76ff.
264. Ibid., 80f.
265. Ibid., 58.
266. Ibid., 31.
267. Ibid.

268. Essentially the following hypotheses have been put forward in connection with the question of its origin; they can be divided into historical and non-historical. The frequency of particular themes is thought to point to either an oriental (e.g. Babylonian) origin, to one from the esoteric circles of heterodox Judaism, to roots in Late Platonism (as a kind of Platonism run wild) or to an origin within the Christian community. Some motives suggest an association of Gnosticism with Buddhism or with Sufism (a mystical branch of Islam). This bewildering abundance of such attempts at derivation, which contradict one another, make it understandable why people have attempted to introduce other than historical criteria. Some scholars want to distil out a Gnostic attitude to existence which then underwent differing developments in different cultural circles. In this connection there is talk of a spiritual basic structure of the Gnostics (according to C.G. Jung: mythical projection of self-experience), in the sociological sense of an answer to the confusing world at the beginning of our era, or laying claim to Martin Heidegger and a philosophy of pessimism which suggested itself from the pressure of historical reality.

269. Pagels explicitly stresses that she wants to leave aside the question of origins but is interested in what can be discovered about the origins of Christianity from the textual evidence of Christian Gnosticism (31). However, it emerges from the book as a whole that Pagels is not in fact as cautious as her explicit interest suggests. As I have said, she holds the Gnostics to be the best Christians.

270. As I am not a Coptologist and therefore can read the Coptic texts only in translation, I took the advice of Dr Robert Haardt in Vienna. I would like to thank him at this point for his long and detailed conversations.

271. On closer inspection this rough classification can be made more precise. There are texts which contain no themes from the circle of Jewish-Christian ideas, texts which have a marked mythological character, and texts which display hardly any mythological features. Some Christian-Gnostic texts seek to be understood as genuinely Christian, others have merely had a Christian revision but, like the Apocryphon of John (see 113f. below), enjoyed great popularity in Christian Gnostic circles. Reality is always more varied than can be grasped by a reflection which investigates 'what', 'whence' and 'why'. That must be remembered in all attempts at making judgments.

272. 'Manichaeism is the concluding and consistent systematization of the Gnosticism of late antiquity in the form of a universal religion of revelation with a missionary character' (R.Haardt, 'Manichäismus', in *Sacramentum Mundi. Theologisches Lexikon für die Praxis*, 1969, [326ff.] 328). The founder of Manichaeism was the aristocrat Mani, who was born in Babylonia in 216.

273. Cf. R.Haardt, *Die Gnosis. Wesen und Zeugnisse*, Salzburg 1967, 10. Haardt points to elements of Gnosticism in mediaeval sects like the Bogomils, Cathari and Albigensians. Cf. R.A.Knox, *Enthusiasm. A Chapter in the History of Religion*, Cambridge University Press 1950.

274. Cf. R.Haardt, 'Mandäismus', in *Sacramentum Mundi*, 322ff. For the textual evidence for Mandaism cf. R.Haardt, *Gnosis*, 265ff.; W.Foerster (ed.), *Die Gnosis 2: Koptische und mandäische Quellen*, Die Bibliothek der alten Welt, Zurich/Stuttgart 1971, 171ff.

275. See above, 26ff.

276. The publications already mentioned each have an introduction giving a short history of the discovery of the Nag Hammadi texts: Pagels, *The Gnostic Gospels*, 13ff.; Haardt, *Die Gnosis*, 337ff.; Foerster, *Die Gnosis*, 7ff.

277. These include e.g. the tractate Poimandres, the Pistis Sophia and the two books of Jeu, the Gospel according to Mary, the Apocryphon of John (short version) and the Sophia Jesu Christi.

278. Precise dating of the Gnostic texts is not always possible and is sometimes disputed. The main areas of Gnostic activity were Syria and Egypt and for a while Rome. The evidence for Simonian Gnosticism, which is named after the Simon Magus mentioned in Acts 8.9ff., falls into the first and second centuries. The Apocryphon of John, Paraphrase of Shem, Gospel of Mary and the literature of the heads of Gnostic schools and teachers Valentinus, Ptolemy, Saturnilus (a pupil of Simon), Basilides and Marcus come from the second century. There is uncertainty over the dating of the Gospel of Thomas, the Gospel of Philip, the Dialogue of the Redeemer and the Book of Thomas the Contender: datings range from the third to the fifth century. Finally the Pistis Sophia is probably a late and dogmatic form of fourth/fifth century Gnosticism, but it too may have been written earlier.

279. Through phrases like: a group of Gnostic texts seeks..., another thinks..., there are those who..., yet others say..., Pagels points out the differences within Christian Gnostic literature, but for the uninitiated reader a tendency to generalization and harmonization prevails.

280. R.Haardt, *Die Gnosis*, 273 n.15, cf. the thesis of K.Korschorke, *Die Polemik der Gnostiker gegen das kirchliche Christentum*, 1978, 181ff., 220ff., etc: 'Gnostic insight seeks to go beyond the church's faith or interpret it in

pneumatic terms but not to replace it; for the Gnostic ,the relationship of church faith to its own insight is represented as one between a limited knowledge and a perfect knowledge, but not as a contrast between wrong and right' (183). Koschorke speaks of the 'ecclesiological model of the inner circle' (220).

281. Cf. W.Foerster, 'Die "ersten Gnostiker" Simon und Menander', in *Le Origini dello Gnosticismo, Colloquio di Messina 1966*, Supplements to Numen XII, 1967, 190ff.

282. Simonianism has been handed on to us only by secondary literature: in addition to Acts also by Justin, Irenaeus, Clement of Alexandria and Epiphanius.

283. Justin, *Apology* I,26,1-3.

284. Ibid.

285. Irenaeus, *Adversus haereses* I,23,2.

286. Ibid., I,23,3.

287. The little evidence that we have about Simon and his followers seems to some scholars not to offer a finished Gnostic system but rather 'unfinished' Gnosticism (thus W.Foerster, *Gnosis*, 195). In contrast to the classical Gnostics, in whose view parts of the supreme divinity had become trapped in matter, Simon and Helen understand themselves as gods and receive worship accordingly (cf. R.Haardt, *Gnosis*, 302). The two evidently appear as a heavenly couple (syzygy: cf.W.A.Meeks, 'The Image of the Androgyne', 191f.; for the idea of syzygies see below, 000f.). But the theme of self-divinization appears more clearly precisely in the fact that Simonian Gnosis to some degree 'goes over the top' (Foerster); this theme is also implied in the conception of a nucleus of divine essence in man.

288. The Egyptian Valentinus was the most influential Gnostic of the second century. He worked for a while in Rome and founded a very influential school; the Valentinians were regarded by the church Christians as the most successful and therefore the most stubborn variant of Gnosticism.

289. As the Gnostics understood it, myth is reality in which human beings have a share. Luise Schottroff works that out well: the tension in Sophia between light and fall, power and lack, innocence and guilt, accords with human experience (*Der Glaubende und die feindliche Welt*, WMANT 37, 1970, 4, etc.). It therefore remains questionable whether the Gnostic myth can be understood among other things as a possible 'objectification' of a general Gnostic understanding of existence, as Korschorke thinks (see n.280), in that he simply defines Gnosticism in terms of the abstract 'escape from the world tendency' (208, etc.; 5f., etc.). Koschorke is very strongly influenced by the polemic against the church fathers which takes the 'vague' myth as an occasion for 'proving' the abstruseness of Gnostic doctrines. 'The tendency to escape from the world' is not just a characteristic of Gnosticism, and Christian-Gnostic texts which have few if any mythological elements share the understanding of reality in the mythological texts.

In Simon it is the female light figure, Ennoia, which falls; in the Valentinian systems it is Sophia; in the Tractate Poimandres, a pagan-Gnostic writing, the sexes of the light-beings are reversed: here the male divine hypostasis Anthropos causes the fall.

290. Thus it is constantly argued that it is an anachronism to determine what is Christian in terms of the victorious party, the orthodox Christians. Had the Gnostic variant prevailed, that would now be regarded as 'Christian'. Pagels also argues that way. However, one must also take into account the tradition as it is, including the Jewish tradition from which the Christian tradition comes. All forms of self-deification by human beings are always rejected and criticized; the

strict separation of the Creator God and any form of creatureliness is among the characteristics of the Jewish-Christian circle of religion. That conversely the controversy of Christians with Gnosticism and above all also with Greek philosophy did not fail to have its influence on the Christians, is in the nature of things. It can be shown again, for example, in Clement of Alexandria: through concern with theology – albeit on the presupposition of faith – 'one becomes like God, I mean God the saviour, in that one shows honour to the God of the universe through the high-priestly Logos' (*Stromateis* II, 45,7). E.Heintel therefore aptly speaks of two forms of theology: one of immanent philosophy and one which is concerned to appropriate in thought the faith presupposed 'in specific positiveness' (*Gott ohne Eigenschaften*, 45f.).

291. Pagels, *The Gnostic Gospels*, 29.

292. Ibid., 20.

293. Ibid., 27, 28; cf. n.268 above.

294. Ibid., 14, 27f.

295. R.Haardt, *Gnosis*, 17.

296. Cf.R.Haardt, 'Gnosis', *Sacramentum Mundi*, 476ff.

297. R.Haardt, *Gnosis*, 16f. Cf. above 00f.

298. Ibid., 11.

299. Pagels, *The Gnostic Gospels*, 71ff.,73.

300. Cf.G.Scholem, *Die jüdische Mystik in ihren Hauptströmungen* (1957) 1980, 38 etc.; from the present perspective we speak of 'abstruse artificial myths'. For the Gnostic, existential problems underlay this, not least the experience of evil in the world. Cf. R.Haardt, 'Schöpfer und Schöpfung in der Gnosis', in *Altes Testament-Frühjudentum-Gnosis*, ed. K.-W.Troger, 1980, 37ff.

301. Three versions of this work, which for example Irenaeus also knows, were found at Nag Hammadi. In my selection of texts I go by Elaine Pagels, because I am challenging her feminist conclusions. But I do not limit myself to short extracts from the text but attempt to assess the significance of the statements from a wider context.

302. Apocryphon of John, Papyrus Berolinensis (BG 21,1), see Hardt, *Gnosis*, 156. Here Jesus is understood as one of the emanations of the supreme God.

303. AJ, Codex II 2.26-4.12, in *Die drei Versionen des Apokryphon des Johannes im koptischen Museum zu Alt-Kairo*, ed. M.Krause and P.Labib, 1962, (16ff.) 13-18. I have basically gone by Codex III, and taken Codex II into account above all because the term Metropator to which Pagels refers occurs by far the most frequently in this codex (see below, 117f.). A convenient collection of texts is *The Nag Hammadi Library in English*, ed.James M.Robinson, E.J.Brill, Leiden 1977, from which translations have been taken where relevant texts are included.

304. This 'negative theology' is rightly seen to have a connection with mysticism (so e.g. Dodds, Scholem, Quispel).

305. Pagels, *The Gnostic Gospels*, 71; but the supreme God is very often called father or primal father in Gnostic texts.

306. C.Schmidt (ed.), *Koptisch-gnostische Schriften* 1.4A, ed. H.M.Schenke, 1981, 333.

307. AJ II, 4.19f.

308. AJ II, 4.26-5.9.

309. AJ Codex III, 7.22-8.5.

310. The text of the *Megale Apophasis* has been handed down to us by Hippolytus (beginning of the third century).

311. *Megale Apophasis*, Hippolytus, *Refutatio* VI.17.3, in Foerster, *Gnosis*, 1, (326ff.), 333; cf. Pagels, *The Gnostic Gospels*, 73.

312. AJ Codex III, 13.11-16, for example, praises Adam, who is also an emanation and belongs to the upper world of light, 'the invisible Spirit, since for your sake all things have come into being for you' (13.12-13): 'I praise you and the autogenes and the aeon, the three: the father, the mother, the son, the complete power' (13.14-16). The concept of 'mother' in this context again refers clearly to the emanations and not to the supreme God.

315. AJ III, 14.9-22. The male-female spirit is singled out from the invisible Spirit, the supreme God and Father, specifically by its androgynous determination as an emanation. In Christianized form it appears as the 'Holy Spirit'; it is called the 'mother of all living' (AJ III, 15.20-1).

316. AJ III, 15.8-16.11.

317. AJ III, 17ff.

318. AJ III, 20,13-32.

319. AJ III, 21,8-11.

320. AJ BG, 37,1.

321. AJ BG 44,1.

322. K.Kokorschke, *Die Polemik der Gnostiker*, 255. The Pistis Sophia was also found among the Nag Hammadi texts (cf. n.277). Kokorschke describes it as follows: 'A dogmatizing of mythology, scholarly concern for tradition on the one hand and a situation of far-reaching isolation from the mainstream of contemporary Christianity on the other...' (255). I mention the writing nevertheless, in order to show that the motives important for our theme maintained themselves over centuries.

323. Pistis Sophia C.30.

324. Ibid.

325. Ibid. C 31.

326. Ibid.

327. We have Ptolemy only in the testimonies of the church fathers (Irenaeus, Clement of Alexandria), as for example his Letter to Flora (Epiphanius).

328. Irenaeus, *Adversus haereses* I.2.1.

329. Ibid., I.4.1.

330. Ibid., I.4.2; I.5.1.

331. Ibid., I.5.3,4.

332. This writing is known to us through the Nag Hammadi texts and has many parallels to AJ, so it is among the Gnostic texts which have undergone a Christian revision. In R.A.Bullard, *The Hypostasis of the Archons*, 1970.

333. Hypostasis of the Archons Table 134.30-135.4., op.cit., 19f.

334. Ibid., 142.4-333, op.cit., 35.

335. Pagels, *The Gnostic Gospels*, 113.

336. Gospel of Thomas 114.

337. Foerster, *Gnosis* II, 139ff.

338. Pagels, *The Gnostic Gospels*, 113.

339. Ibid.

340. The Dialogue of the Redeemer, a writing from the Nag Hammadi complex, shows that asceticism and repudiation of the feminine can go with a high estimation of women (here again Mary Magdalene). Moreover, here Mary again appears as Jesus's heavenly consort.

341. Pagels, *The Gnostic Gospels*, 113.

342. Ibid.

343. Cf.Irenaeus, *Adversus haereses* I.2.5.
344. AJ III 28.21.
345. AJ III 31.6-32.3 (31.21-32.3).
346. The attitude of the Gnostics to marriage ranges from virtually aggressive asceticism to the concession of marriage for those who have not yet attained complete knowledge. The difference from Paul, who also concedes marriage, lies in motivation: Paul is concerned for freedom for service in the Gospel; the Gnostics want to starve the world, the domination of evil power, into surrender. Moreover Paul does not distinguish classes of men but gifts of grace. Here again are signs of the danger when one only keeps to the themes of asceticism and concession and does not see the overall context in which these themes stand.
347. This notion occurs in the Gospel of Philip, which is mentioned by Epiphanius, who cites a short section of it; it is probably not identical with the Gospel of Philip found at Nag Hammadi, as this quotation does not appear there. Possibly there were two Gospels of the same name. Quotation from Epiphanius in E.Hennecke, W.Stuhlmacher and R.McL.Wilson, *New Testament Apocrypha* I, 1963. 273.
348. Pagels, *The Gnostic Gospels*, 86.
349. Satornilus (Saturninus) is mentioned by the church fathers in connection with Basilides (at the end of the first, beginning of the second century). Neither knows a Sophia myth but they do know an anthropos myth. The God of the Old Testament is not evil, like the demiurge, but is not identical with the supreme unknown God either.
350. Irenaeus, *Adversus haereses*, I.24.2.
351. Ibid.
353. Basilides has been handed down to us through the church fathers (above all Clement of Alexandria and Origen). His system is characterized *inter alia* by the conception of a migration of souls and the rejection of the notion of emanation: according to Basilides the evil demiurge repents when he hears the Gospel. The Basilidians can be found until the fourth century.
354. Clement of Alexandria, *Stromateis* III.1.1-3.
355. See above, n.278.
356. Gospel of Thomas 11.
357. Ibid., 22.
358. Ibid., 56.
359. Ibid., 79.
360. Ibid., 114.
361. Gospel of Philip in Epiphanius (see n.347): mankind incurs guilt through procreation because through it light again enters into the captivity of matter. K.Koschorke, *Die Polemik der Gnostiker*, 123ff., gives a wealth of evidence about Gnostic sexual asceticism,
362. For the accusation of libertinism cf. K.Koschorke, op.cit.; K.Niederwimmer, *Askese und Mysterium*, 200ff.; H.Kraft, *Gnostisches Gemeinschaftsleben*, typescript dissertation, Heidelberg 1950, 156ff. R.Haardt, *Die Gnosis*, 15f.
363. Pistis Sophia C.147.
364. Koschorke, *Die Polemik der Gnostiker*, 231f.
365. Epiphanius, *Panarion* 26.4.3-8; 5.4-5.
366. Epiphanius distinguishes between two works, the Great Questions of Mary and the Little Questions of Mary, cf. *NT Apocrypha*, I, 338f.
367. Epiphanius, *Panarion* 26.8.2.

368. Cf. W.Maleczek, 'Kirche und Ketzer im Mittelalter', in *Schulfach Religion*, ed. W.Frank and S.Heine, Vol.1/2, 1982, (63ff.) 70f.

369. Cf. H.Grundmann, *Religiöse Bewegungen im Mittelalter*, ²1961.

370. H.Kraft, *Gnostisches Gemeinschaftsleben*, 128f.

371. Ibid., 156.

372. Ibid., 120ff.

373. Irenaeus, *Adversus haereses* I.21.3.

374. Gospel of Philip 78. Here this is the Gospel of Philip from Nag Hammadi, cf. Foerster, *Gnosis*, 2 (95ff.), 111.

375. Gospel of Philip 122.

376. Ibid., 61.

377. H.Kraft, *Gnostisches Gemeinschaftsleben*, points to the attempt to avoid erotic associations by the choice of particular terms. Thus the feminine part of the couple is not called sister, as among Christians, but syzygos, literally yoke companion, i.e. a companion with which one is linked under the same yoke as with an oxen.

378. Pagels, *The Gnostic Gospels*, 84. Whether the significance of Mary Magdalene in the Gnostic texts corresponds to her historical significance in the community can no longer be reconstructed unless new texts appear which give us more information.

379. Cf. *New Testament Apocrypha* I, 257.

380. Pistis Sophia C.146. The opposition between Mary and Peter is not to be understood in historical terms. The Gnostics regarded Peter as the representative of church Christianity (legalistic!) to which the Gnostic felt superior. Mary by contrast stands for the Gnostic position (thus in the Gospel of Thomas, the Gospel of Mary and the Pistis Sophia): K.Koschorke, *Gnostisches Gemeinschaftsleben*, 33 n.27.

381. See above, 126f.

382. The Gospel according to Mary is to be found (incomplete) in Papyrus Berolinensis (see n.302) and comes from the second century.

383. *New Testament Apocrypha* 1, 343.

384. Gospel of Philip, 55.

385. See above, 55.

386. Gospel of Philip, 32.

387. Thus in the Gospel of Mary and the Pistis Sophia.

388. Gospel of Philip, 55; cf. W.A.Meeks, 'The Image of the Androgyne', 190.

389. Cf.e.g. Kraft, *Gnostisches Gemeinsamleben*; Pagels, *The Gnostic Gospels*, 80ff.

390. Pagels, *The Gnostic Gospels*, 105.

391. See above 83f.

392. See above, 29f.

393. R.A Knox, *Enthusiasm*, 20.

394. C.Honegger, *Die Hexen der Neuzeit*, 1979, Introduction, (21ff.) 39.

395. J.B.Russell, 'Hexerei und Geist des Mittelalters', in op.cit., (259ff.) 173.

396. Celsus, in Origen, *Contra Celsum* (see n.79).

397. Cf. the basic notions in S.Heine, 'Zeitgeist und Gottesgeist', *Amt und Gemeinde* 5, 1986, 45f.

398. Tertullian, *Apology* 41. Cf. *On Baptism* 17.

399. Kraft, *Gnostisches Gemeinschaftsleben*, 146.

400. The Marcusians are named after Marcus, a pupil of Valentinus, who was

active in Asia Minor in the second half of the second century. He had a tendency towards magic and more popular forms of Gnosticism.

401. Irenaeus, *Adversus haereses* I,13.2.

402. Ibid.

403. Ibid.

404. See 31 above.

405. For Apelles, too, evil in the world and the flesh do not derive from the creation of the supreme good God but from a fallen angel; Apelles advocates celibacy.

406. Marcellina gathered a community around herself in Rome and combined a wealth of religious and philosophical themes in her teaching. Whether Carpocrates was a historical person or not can no longer be determined.

407. H.Kraft, *Gnostisches Gemeinschaftsleben*, 151.

408. For the anti-hierarchical structure of Gnostic communities cf. Kraft, op.cit., 149f.; Pagels, *The Gnostic Gospels*, 65ff.; K.Koschorke, *Die Polemik der Gnostiker*, 67ff.

409. The Tripartite Tractate is Valentinian and a good example of the negative theology of the Gnostics.

410. Pagels, *The Gnostic Gospels*, 65. The self-understanding of the Gnostics very probably included the conviction that they were better Christians; but this cannot be understood in terms of an exalted sense of status but is the result of a knowledge which is not in principle possible for all. The others have not got so far. Koschorke thinks that the model of the 'inner circle' serves to answer the question 'how the hearers could respond in such different ways to the preaching of the Saviour' (op.cit., 226f.).

411. See n.272 above.

412. Augustine, *De haeresibus ad Quodvultdeum* 46.4. The *electae* are more detached towards the Christian community than for example the pneumatics among the Valentinians. Thinking in terms of qualitatively different 'classes of men' takes on differing contours among the Gnostics.

413. The Manichaeans also regard marriage in principle as reprehensible, but it is conceded to hearers of a lower status.

414. Here is an example: 'If through misunderstanding we should have committed any offence against the holy dintars (= elect) who occupy themselves with good works and redemption, and if although we called them true messengers of God and prophets we have not believed in them... my God, we now repent and ask for forgiveness of our sins' (R.Haardt, *Gnosis*, 244f.).

415. Kraft, *Gnostisches Gemeinschaftsleben*, 146.

416. For the problem of pseudepigraphy see n.22.

417. The assessment of everyday ethics is virtually the most disputed point: the range extends from the petty bourgeois spirit as a betrayal of the kingdom of heaven to the predicate of nobility for Christianity (cf. K.Berger, *Exegese des Neuen Testaments*, 239). See below 144f.

418. P.Vielhauer, *Geschichte der urchristlichen Literatur*, 1975, 229.

419. See above, 86f.

420. Cf.G.Fitzer, *Das Weib schweige in der Gemeinde*, Theologische Existenz heute 110, 1963, and the criticism of Fitzer's method by G.Dautzenberg, *Die Frau im Urchristentum*, 193f., though Dautzenberg *de facto* comes to the same conclusion as Fitzer.

421. See above, 88f.

422. Cf. G.Lohfink, 'Weibliche Diakone im Neuen Testament', in *Die Frau im*

Urchristentum, 332ff.; N.Brox, *Die Pastoralbriefe*, Regensburger NT ⁴1969, 154.

423. The heyday of the diaconate of women as a church office is in the third century.

424. Brox, *Die Pastoralbriefe*, 189.

425. The house tables always relate to all the members of the house, including children and slaves. However, here we are only interested in relationships between the married couple.

426. From K.Müller, 'Die Haustafel des Kolosserbriefes und das antike Frauenthema', in *Die Frau im Urchristentum*, (263ff.) 297.

427. Ibid., 298.

428. Ibid., 317.

429. Ibid., 318.

430. As the heretics appeal to the spirit, and prophecy is therefore valued highly among them, prophetic speech is regarded by the heresy hunters as the point of entry for false teaching. Here too repudiation is a decisive reason for the loss.

431. That is not to express any value judgment. Cf. n.417; on the judgment cf. 000f. below.

432. Brox, *Die Pastoralbriefe*, 51.

433. Cf.E.Moltmann-Wendel, *The Women around Jesus*, 138, though she exaggerates.

434. See above, 131f.

435. Brox, *Die Pastoralbriefe*, 125.

436. K.Thraede, *Ärger der Freiheit*, 124.

437. See n.280.

438. That applies above all to the Valentinians, cf. Koschorke, *Die Polemik der Gnostiker*, 175ff.

439. Cf. op.cit., 228, 248f.

440. Ibid., 238f.

441. See above, 139.

442. Cf. Koschorke, *Die Polemik der Gnostiker*, 231.

443. Cf. K.Koschorke, 'Eine neugefundene gnostiche Gemeindeordnung', *ZTK* 76, 1979, 30ff.

444. Apocalypse of Peter 79.21-31, a text from Nag Hammadi, third century.

445. Ibid., 77ff.

446. Tertullian, for example, writes polemic against this understanding in his work on baptism, and he attempts to justify its sacramental significance by means of the value of the element of water.

447. Cf. K.Koschorke, *Die Polemik der Gnostiker*, 142f.

448. For unjustified disparagement of myth cf. n.273.

449. Cf. Koschorke, op.cit., 123ff.

450. Ibid., 115.

451. Ibid., 117.

452. Polemic against the Gnostics skilled in the Bible also leads, for example, to devaluing the significance of the Bible for the community.

453. Koschorke, 'Eine neugefundene gnostische Gemeindeordnung', 37f.

454. Koschorke, *Die Polemik der Gnostiker*, 252f.

455. There is, however, clear consensus about this.

456. E.Schüssler-Fiorenza, 'Der Beitrag der Frau', 79.

457. Cf. e.g. K.Berger, *Exegese des Neuen Testaments*, 245, etc., and K.Nieder-wimmer, *Askese und Mysterium*, 220ff.

458. Cf. N.Luhmann, in *Zwischen Technologie und Selbstreferenz*, ed. N.Luhmann and E.Schorr, 1982. Luhmann is concerned with the question of 'the possibility of reconciling empirical causality and freedom'.

Index of Biblical References

Index of Names